T. D. Jakes Enterprises Presents

In the Multitude of Counsel

Legal Strategies For the 21st Century Church

Curtis W. Wallace, Esq.

General Editor

Contributions By:

Dr. Ted Baehr, Esq.

Dr. Dan Beirute, Esq.

Curtis W. Wallace, Esq.

Thomas G. Gehring, Esq.

David O. Middlebrook, Esq.

Thomas Winters, Esq.

A Multitude of Counsel

Legal Strategies For the 21st Century Church

ISBN 1-57855-625-2

Copyright © 2001 by Curtis W. Wallace

5787 S. Hampton Road, Suite 445, LB 125

Dallas, Texas 75232-2200

Published by T. D. Jakes Enterprises, Inc.

5787 S. Hampton Road, Suite 445, LB 125

Dallas, TX 75232-2200

Printed by Integrity Concepts, Tulsa, OK

Table of Contents

Acknowledgements

With any significant understanding, success is not possible without people. All of the people who played a role in this effort have positively impacted both the book and myself.

To Bishop T. D. Jakes, a very special thanks for all of the roles you play in my life. In addition to mentor, employer and friend, we can now add publisher. You da man!

To Nat Tate, your friendship and partnership are greatly appreciated. Your encouragement convinced me to undertake this book.

To Rosilyn, Keith, Derrick, Trina, Sherri and the entire T. D. Jakes Enterprises team, thank you for your support. You are the best team that I have ever worked with.

To my beautiful wife Julaina, you make me a better man. Without you, nothing I have done would have been possible. You are simply the best part of me.

To my sons Jackson, Harrison and Carter, thank you for your unconditional love.

Finally, I want to thank my parents Jimmy and Joyce Wallace for supporting me in everything I have ever wanted to do.

Curtis W. Wallace

Special Thanks to the Multitude of Counsel

The title of this book is A Multitude of Counsel. That title is purposeful and significant. The book is the result of a collaborative effort among six lawyers — Thomas G. Gehring, Ted Baehr, Thomas J. Winters, Dan Beirute, David O. Middlebrook and myself.

Without the efforts and insights of any one of the contributors, this book would not be the first quality work that I believe it to be.

Tom Gehring, Ted Baehr, Tom Winters, Dan Beirute and David Middlebrook are all exceptional lawyers and better people. Thanks to each of you for your help and support.

Curtis W. Wallace

Preface

Where no counsel is, the people fall; but in a multitude of counselors there is safety.
PROVERBS 11:14

Without counsel purposes are disappointed; but in the multitude of counselors they are established.
PROVERBS 15:22

Two are better than one and three are better than two. No matter what the issue is to be addressed and no matter what the problem is to be solved, there is wisdom in seeking the counsel of others. No one person, no matter how experienced or wise has all of the answers. The world is far too complicated to go it alone.

In addition to fulfilling my desire to provide clear cogent advise and understanding to ministries concerning a series of important legal matters, this book has two underlying primary purposes. The first is to make the point that the worlds of law and business are incredibly complex. However, these worlds can be managed and exploited for the good of the Kingdom of God — if you use your gifts, your talents, your instincts, and seek a multitude of counsel. In this complex modern world, no one advisor has all of the answers. That is why four different lawyers contributed to this work. While each contributor has tremendous experience representing ministries, we each have different perspectives, backgrounds, and areas of expertise. By coming together, we have provided, in a single work, the benefit of a multitude of counsel.

The second underlying purpose of this book is to help you understand lawyers. According to Proverbs 15:22, ìin the multitude of counselors [purposes] are established.î This statement personifies the true purpose and objective that your lawyer, your counselor, should have in mind. The goal and objective of each contributor is to aid you, and your ministry, in establishing the purpose for which you have been called.

Over the course of the last several years, I have had the privilege of representing many churches and ministries, both large and small. I have also been directly involved in one of the country's largest and fastest growing ministries. During that time, it occurred to me that churches and the people who run them would benefit tremendously from an understanding of many of the legal strategies employed by cutting edge ministry. Unfortunately, typically only the largest organizations can afford the best legal counsel. Too often the organizations that most needed the help, had the least access to that help.

Thus, this book was born out of a perceived need for a practical legal guide for pastors and church administrators. The intent of the book is to provide the reader with practical, insightful information concerning the legal aspects of running a church or ministry. By understanding and implementing a few simple legal principles, any church can avoid most of the common legal pitfalls encountered in today's world.

As this is intended as a practical, useful book, it is written by a lawyer but not for lawyers. This book highlights the potential problems that a pastor or an administrator needs to be aware of , discussed in clear language, offering practical advice.

My hope is that this book saves you tens of thousands of dollars in legal fees by doing two things. First, the book should help you learn when and how to hire lawyers. Next, by providing basic legal understanding on a few important topics, you will learn when you need to hire lawyers. Some ministries waste money by having a lawyer do something the client could do alone. More often, ministries spend vast sums in legal fees in an attempt to fix a problem that could have been easily solved by paying a much smaller amount in legal fees early on before a crisis had arisen. In these respects, I hope that you find the purchase price to be an investment that brings you significant returns.

This book contains basic information only and is not intended as a comprehensive legal treatise that answers every question. Therefore, it is critical that the reader understands and appreciate that the first rule of law is that every rule has at least one exception. Therefore, if you learn anything from this book, understand that there are no absolutes in the world of law.

CHAPTER ONE

HOW TO FORM AND MAINTAIN
A NON-PROFIT CORPORATION

Curtis W. Wallace

The moment has come. You know what God wants you to do and now you have decided that the season has arrived and it is time for you to start a new church or ministry. The question is, "What do you do next?" The legal answer is easy; you need to form a non-profit corporation through which you will operate your church or ministry.

What is a corporation

A corporation is simply an entity that the law has created so that a group of people can operate a common enterprise together for a common objective. The law allows people to form an entity, called a corporation, so that the enterprise — be it a church, oil company or car wash — can have its own existence separate and apart from the people who operate the enterprise.

This separate existence provides a corporation with two distinct advantages. First, a corporation will provide you with personal legal protection against liability. Because the corporation has a separate legal existence from the people who run it, as a general matter, the corporation, not the people who operate the corporation, is accountable for the actions of the corporation. In other words, the corporation acts as a legal shield of protection for the individuals involved in running the church.

Here is a quick example. Assume that the church bus is involved in an accident and that the accident was caused by Elder Brown, a church employee, and that Bob Jones, the driver of the other vehicle involved in the accident is seriously injured and incurs several thousand dollars in medical bills and is off work for six months. Bob Jones is going to want somebody to pay. Without the protection of a corporation, Pastor Wilson who runs the church, but was no where near the accident, is likely to be the one who gets sued by Bob Jones. If a corporation exists, it will be the corporation that gets sued.

Similar rules apply to the debts and obligations of the church. If the corporation incurred the debts, the corporation alone is liable for those debts (unless some individual personally guaranteed the debt). Clearly, the separate existence and legal shield afforded by forming a corporation are extremely beneficial.

Second, forming a non-profit corporation will make it much easier for your church to enjoy the advantages of being tax-exempt. While it is possible for a church to operate on a tax-exempt basis without forming a corporation, it is often difficult. Businesses and governmental agencies particularly are used to dealing with corporate entities. Forming a non-profit corporation makes it very clear what your organization is. As a result, filing for and obtaining various exemptions for sales taxes, property taxes and the like will be greatly eased.

At this point, it is clear that you need to form a non-profit corporation, if you have not already done. Accordingly, this chapter will walk you through, step by step, the process of forming a non-profit corporation to house your church or ministry.

For the majority of you who are managing an existing non-profit corporation, this chapter will aid you in understanding how your corporation functions as an entity. As a pastor or administrator, you need to have a solid understanding of your organization's structure and rules. Without that knowledge, you are vulnerable to a multitude of potential pitfalls and problems. When you finish this chapter, you will be able to quickly analyze your own corporate structure and, more importantly, determine if that structure is appropriate for your situation and, finally, work with your lawyer to put the proper structure in place.

In addition, this chapter will detail the steps necessary to maintain your corporation in good standing with the governmental authorities. You will learn the steps that need to be followed so that your corporation will continue to exist and, thereby, provide you with all of the benefits and protections that a corporate structure is intended to provide.

When reading this chapter, think of your corporation as the foundation upon which your organization is built. If you have a solid foundation comprised of a sound corporate structure and well thought-out corporate practices, your ministry will be on firm ground. On the other hand, cracks in your corporate foundation are very likely to lead to bigger problems in the rest of your house.

How to form a non-profit corporation

Today, the actual process of forming a non-profit corporation is a relatively quick and simple three-step process. Once a few key decisions have been made, most lawyers can complete the paperwork in a day or two. First, Articles of Incorporation (also called a Certificate of Incorporation in some states) are prepared and filed with the designated state official, typically the Secretary of State in the state where you want to incorporate. Once the Secretary of State has accepted the Articles of Incorporation for filing, the corporation begins to exist as a separate entity. Second, Bylaws (some people refer to Bylaws as a Constitution) for the newly formed corporation must be adopted. The Bylaws set forth the rules for the operation of the corporation. Finally, an initial meeting of the Board of Directors of the newly formed corporation must be held to approve its formation, adopt the Bylaws as its own, elect officers and take care of a few other housekeeping matters. Once these three steps are completed, you will have an operational non-profit corporation.

However, before the appropriate documents can be prepared, a number of decisions will need to be made. There is no "one size fits all" non-profit corporation. As a result, you will need to tailor the structure of your corporation to fit your particular needs.

To assist in deciding how to tailor your organization, a sample Articles of Incorporation has been provided with a discussion and explanation of each section following.

Articles of Incorporation

ARTICLES OF INCORPORATION/PRIVATE
OF GLOBAL CHURCH, INC.

I, the undersigned natural person over the age of eighteen (18), acting as an incorporator, adopt the following Articles of Incorporation of GLOBAL CHURCH, INC. (referred to as the "Corporation") under the Texas Non-Profit Corporation Act (referred to as the "Act"):

ARTICLE 1

NAME

The name of the Corporation is GLOBAL CHURCH, INC.

ARTICLE 2

NONPROFIT CORPORATION

The Corporation is a nonprofit corporation. Upon dissolution, all of the Corporation's assets shall be distributed to an organization exempt from taxes under Internal Revenue Code Section 501(c)(3) for one or more purposes.

ARTICLE 3

DURATION

The Corporation shall continue in perpetuity.

ARTICLE 4

PURPOSES

The Corporation is organized exclusively to perform charitable, educational and religious activities within the meaning of Internal Revenue Code Section 501(c)(3). Specifically, the Corporation is organized to spread the gospel of Jesus Christ by all means possible throughout the world.

ARTICLE 5

POWERS

Except as otherwise provided in these Articles, the Corporation shall have all of the powers provided in the Act. Moreover, the Corporation shall have all implied powers necessary and proper to carry out its express powers. The Corporation may pay reasonable compensation to directors, or officers for services rendered to or for the Corporation in furtherance of one or more of its purposes set forth above.

ARTICLE 6

RESTRICTIONS AND REQUIREMENTS

The Corporation shall not pay dividends or other corporate income to its directors or officers or otherwise accrue distributable profits or permit the realization of private gain. The Corporation shall have no power to take any action prohibited by the Act. The Corporation shall not have the power to engage in any activities, except to an insubstantial degree, that are not in furtherance of the purposes set forth above. The Corporation shall have no power to take any action that would be inconsistent with the requirements for a tax exemption under Internal Revenue Code Section 501(c)(3) and related regulations, rulings, and procedures. The Corporation shall have no power to take any action that would be inconsistent with the requirements for receiving tax-deductible charitable contributions under Internal Revenue Code Section 170(c)(2) and related regulations, rulings, and procedures. Regardless of any other provision in these Articles of Incorporation or state law, the Corporation shall have no power to:

1. Engage in activities or use its assets in manners that are not in furtherance of one or more exempt purposes, as set forth above and defined by the Internal Revenue Code and related regulations, rulings, and procedures, except to an insubstantial degree.

2. Serve a private interest other than one that is clearly incidental to an overriding public interest.

3. Devote more than an insubstantial part of its activities to attempting to influence legislation by propaganda or otherwise, except as provided by the Internal Revenue Code and related regulations, rulings, and procedures.

4. Participate in or intervene in any political campaign on behalf of or in opposition to any candidate for public office. The prohibited activities include the publishing or distributing of statements and any other direct or indirect campaign activities.

5. Have objectives that characterize it as an "action organization" as defined by the Internal Revenue Code and related regulations, rulings, and procedures.

6. Distribute its assets on dissolution other than for one or more exempt purposes; on dissolution, the Corporation's assets shall be distributed to the state government for a public purpose, or to an organization exempt from taxes under Internal Revenue Code Section 501(c)(3) to be used to accomplish the general purposes for which the Corporation was organized.

7. Permit any part of the net earnings of the Corporation to inure to the benefit of any private shareholder or member of the Corporation or any private individual.

8. Carry on an unrelated trade or business except as a secondary purpose related to the Corporation's primary, exempt, purposes.

ARTICLE 7

MEMBERSHIP

The Corporation shall have no members. [The Corporation shall have members with the rights and powers as specified in the Bylaws of the Corporation].

ARTICLE 8

INITIAL REGISTERED OFFICE AND AGENT

The street address of the initial registered office of the Corporation is [INSERT ADDRESS OF THE CORPORATION'S REGISTERED AGENT - IT MUST BE A PHYSICAL STREET ADDRESS]. The name of the initial registered agent at this office is [INSERT NAME OF THE REGISTERED AGENT - MAY BE A PERSON OR A CORPORATION].

ARTICLE 9

BOARD OF DIRECTORS

The qualifications, manner of selection, duties, terms, and other matters relating to the Board of Directors (referred to as the "Board of Directors") shall be provided in the bylaws. The initial Board of Directors shall consist of [INSERT THE NUMBER OF INITIAL BOARD MEMBERS - MUST BE 3 OR MORE] persons. The number of directors may be increased or decreased by amendment of bylaws. The number of directors may not be decreased to less than three. The initial Board of Directors shall consist of the following persons at the following addresses:

Name of DirectorStreet Address

[INSERT NAME][INSERT ADDRESS]

[INSERT NAME][INSERT ADDRESS]

[INSERT NAME][INSERT ADDRESS]

ARTICLE 10

LIMITATION ON LIABILITY OF DIRECTORS

A director is not liable to the Corporation or members for monetary damages for an act or omission in the director's capacity as director except to the extent otherwise provided by a statute of the State of Texas.

ARTICLE 11

INDEMNIFICATION

The Corporation may indemnify a person who was, is, or is threatened to be made a named defendant or respondent in litigation or other proceedings because the person is or was a director or other person related to the Corporation as provided by the provisions in the Act governing indemnification. As provided in the bylaws, the Board of Directors shall have the power to define the requirements and limitations for the Corporation to indemnify directors, officers, or others related to the Corporation. ARTICLE 12

CONSTRUCTION

All references in these Articles of Incorporation to statutes, regulations, or other sources of legal authority shall refer to the authorities cited, or their successors, as they may be amended from time to time.

ARTICLE 13

INCORPORATORS

The name and street address of the incorporator is:

Name of IncorporatorAddress

Curtis W. Wallace

ARTICLE 14

ACTION BY WRITTEN CONSENT

Action may be taken by use of signed written consents by the number of members, directors, or committee members whose vote would be necessary to take action at a meeting at which all such persons entitled to vote were present and voted. Each written consent must bear the date of signature of each person signing it. A consent signed by less than all of the members, directors, or committee members is not effective to take the intended action unless consents, signed by the required number of persons, are delivered to the corporation within 60 days after the date of the earliest dated consent delivered to the corporation. Delivery must be made by hand, or by certified or registered mail, return receipt requested. The delivery may be made to the corporation's registered office, registered agent, principal place of business, transfer agent, registrar, exchange agent, or an officer or agent having custody of books in which the relevant proceedings are recorded. If the delivery is made to the corporation's principal place of business, the consent must be addressed to the president or principal executive officer.

The corporation will give prompt notice of the action taken to persons who do not sign consents. If the action taken requires documents to be filed with the secretary of state, the filed documents will indicate that the written consent procedures have been properly followed.

A telegram, telex, cablegram, or similar transmission by a member, director, or committee member, or photographic, facsimile, or similar reproduction of a signed writing is to be regarded as being signed by the member, director, or committee member.

I execute these Articles of Incorporation on _____,.

The following examines and explains each section of the sample

Articles of Incorporation. This discussion illustrates the options and possibilities that are available to you in creating your corporation.

Article 1

Name

First, you need to pick a name for your new corporation. Prior to talking to your lawyer, I suggest picking several names (at least 3 or 4) and ranking them in order from favorite to least favorite. Then, your lawyer can do a search to see if a particular name is available in your state before the documents are prepared and filed. Please note that when you file Articles of Incorporation with a particular name, it does not mean that you "own" that name. It only means that no one else in your state can use that name for a corporation. To protect your new corporate name, you will also need to file a trademark application with the federal government. One note on names, the more unique the better in terms of being able to protect that name. Common names are very difficult to protect. The name of a church or ministry, and the ability to protect it, can be very significant in the modern world. Today, more and more ministries have a significant media presence and sell a significant amount of product through a variety of distribution outlets. As such, these ministries become "brands" that have value. You should talk with your lawyer at the outset about protecting your ministry's name.

Article 2

Non-profit Corporation.

While very short and relatively simple, this section is probably the most important part of the Articles of Incorporation for you to understand. On the surface, this section simply specifies that the corporation being formed is a non-profit corporation, as opposed to a for-profit stock corporation. In addition, this section specifies that upon dissolution of the corporation (when the corporation is closed down) all of its assets will go to another tax-exempt corporation. You can specify a particular recipient, but because things and people change, I suggest leaving this open-ended. That way, the Board of Directors of your corporation can decide where the assets go when the church or ministry is closed down.

However, in order to properly manage your non-profit corporation, you must understand the underlying significance of this section — THIS IS A NON-PROFIT CORPORATION! A non-profit corporation is one that is not designed to create profits to distribute to its owners. It is not that your non-profit corporation cannot take more money than it spends and, thereby earn a "profit." If you do not do that, you will not survive long. The important point is that "profits" are not distributed to owners, because there are no OWNERS.

IBM is owned by thousands of shareholders who all benefit when IBM's profits increase. However, a non-profit corporation, such as your church or United Way, is not owned by anyone. Instead, non-profit corporation exist for the benefit of the public at large — not any specific individuals.

In essence, our local, state and federal governments have made a deal. The deal is that in exchange for the tax-exempt status that is granted to most non-profits (yes it is possible to be a non-profit, but taxable corporation), non-profits cannot be owned by any individual. Instead, the tax savings need to be used for an allowed purpose that the government has decided benefits society in general (look at the purposes listed in Article 4 of the Articles of Incorporation).

The implication of this concept is immense. Because no one, not even the founding pastor, owns any part of the non-profit corporation, no one should conduct themselves as if they do own it. The corporation exists for the public benefit and should be treated as such. This means that the corporation's assets cannot be used as if they belong to an individual. A non-profit corporation cannot freely distribute its assets to people. It can only pay fair value for goods and services received. This means its employees can earn a fair salary and benefits in exchange for their efforts, but that it is it. No profit sharing plans here.

Why then, would you form a non-profit corporation instead of a for-profit corporation? The answer is simple, tax and donations. Most non-profits, including all churches are exempt from most taxes such as property, sales and income taxes. Moreover, non-profits can receive donations and the donors can take a tax deduction for the amount of the donation.

In other words, the government has chosen to give up billions in tax revenue, but the trade-off is that non-profit corporations have to be operated for the benefit of the public, not individuals. So when you complain about the regulations imposed on churches and other non-profits, remember the deal. You can get rid of the regulation anytime you want, as long as you are ready to pay the taxes and give up the donations.

Moreover, churches should carefully monitor their own activities. There is no constitutional prohibition on the taxation of churches. As long as all churches were equally treated, there is nothing to prevent Congress, other than the political will of the people, from removing tax exemptions. At various times, such efforts have been considered by state and local governments and the IRS frequently voices concern over tax exemptions. The point is that a few very public displays of abuse of the tax-exemption system could lead to calls for further regulation or, theoretically, outright repeal of tax-exemptions.

Article 3

Duration

Corporations can have a perpetual existence and there is no reason to put a limitation in place.

Article 4

Purpose

The purpose statement serves two needs. First, it sets forth why the corporation should be non-profit and entitled to tax-exempt status. For tax exemption purposes, you will need to list those purposes that make your corporation eligible for tax-exemption. Under the Internal Revenue Code, tax-exempt corporations may be formed for religious, educational, scientific, or charitable purposes. While these are very broad terms, "religious," "charitable," "educational," and "scientific" each have specific meanings under the tax code. I suggest that you include religious, charitable, and educational as the purposes for the formation of the corporation. Using those three designations will cover practically any activity that a church or ministry may engage in.

For example, "religious" covers all of your basic ministry related activities that are designed to spread the Gospel. "Educational" will cover a school and "charitable" will cover any benevolent activities undertaken by the church, such as food programs.

Second, the purpose statements set forth what the corporation was formed to do. I suggest a very broad statement such as "to spread the gospel of Jesus Christ by any means possible." Such a broad statement covers any activity in which a church may engage. The point is to avoid the necessity of having to later re-write your Articles of Incorporation.

Whether you include a simple statement or prepare something more elaborate, just remember that the document will be public record. Anyone who so desires can obtain a copy of your Articles of Incorporation. Keep this in mind.

Article 5

Powers

In this section, the powers of the corporation are listed. While some lawyers try to list every imaginable thing that a church corporation might do, something inevitably gets left out. Therefore, I simply state that the corporation has all powers available under law. Again, broad, general statements help avoid the need for later revisions.

If your existing corporation has a very specific Powers or Purpose statement, you may want to consider a revision to ensure that all of your current and planned activities are covered.

Article 6

Restrictions/Requirements

This section includes language that the IRS likes to have included in the Articles of Incorporation. If you comply with these restrictions, you will operate your church or ministry in compliance with the essence of the regulations that govern non-profit corporations. Basically, these rules all come down to the fact that you need to operate your ministry for its exempt purposes and not for the benefit of any individual. The restrictions are dealt with in more detail in Chapter 2.

However, everything in Article 6 goes back to the concept that individuals do not own a non-profit corporation. The public at large is the beneficiary of the corporation's assets. Therefore, you need to keep in mind that the best interest of the organization should be placed ahead of the best interest of the individuals who operate the ministry or church. As a result, any dealings between a non-profit corporation and those people who control it must be fair and at arms-length.

Take a quick look at #3 and #4 under Article 6 (page s 13-14). These rules do not mean that you need to completely avoid political activities. However, follow this simple rule of thumb — It is ok to encourage your congregation to be politically active (telling the church members to be sure to vote next Tuesday in the election); and it is ok to teach whether a particular act is right or wrong (telling the church your views on an issue such as abortion); but it is not ok to tell your church who to vote for and it is not ok for the church to expend its funds on political causes or candidates.

Remember, you, as an individual, are separate from the church as an entity. Therefore, the pastor can give his or her personal money to a candidate. A minister can support or endorse a candidate — they just should not do it from the pulpit.

If you are going to permit political candidates to visit your church,

I suggest that you invite the candidates from both parties. In addition, there is no problem with inviting office holders to special events, such as dedications or anniversaries. An invitation or an appearance by a political office holder is not an endorsement. Just keep the issues separate.

Having said that, I encourage all church leaders to take the time to get to know and develop relationships with governmental leaders at all levels. Any large church will find itself frequently doing business with the government, especially your city and county officials. When doing so, there is no substitute for relationships.

When it comes to dealing with the government, churches generally operate at a significant disadvantage. Governments need tax revenue to operate and churches do not pay taxes. This simple fact means that churches, from a financial standpoint, are liabilities, not assets, to a city government. Therefore, some cities can be less than accommodating to churches. The best way to overcome this setback is to develop relationships. This takes time and effort, but it always pays off.   Article 7

Membership

Non-profit corporations come in two basic types, with or without members. Therefore, the Articles will need to include a statement as to whether or not the corporation will have members. Then, if the corporation has members, the rights of those members will be set out at some point (usually in the corporation's bylaws).

Many church organizations will have members and the Articles of Incorporation of the church generally provide that the members possess only those rights designated in the bylaws. The extent of those rights will depend on the type of organizational structure that the particular church chooses. The general options are discussed below in the section on bylaws.

For a pure ministry (a religious organization that does not operate a church), there is typically no need to have members and a simple statement to that effect is included in the Articles.

The section below on bylaws includes a detailed discussion of the basic organizational structures that most churches or ministries follow.

Article 8

Registered Agent

The Articles will need to list the name and street address (post office boxes are not allowed) of the person who will serve as the registered agent of the corporation. This person will serve two primary functions. First, this individual will be the addressee of any official mail from the state. Therefore, the name and address must be good because the state will assume that any mailed documents were in fact received. Second, this person will most likely be the person who is served with any lawsuit that is filed against the church. Therefore, use a trustworthy individual and an address that is not likely to change often (the address of the church is usually better than the address of an individual). When the person or address changes, you simply need to file a change form with the Secretary of State and pay a small fee.

This simple issue creates more problems for churches that almost any other corporate matter. Most states will periodically send out "public information" forms to all corporations. The forms are mailed to the registered agent at the registered address and are required to be completed and returned within a specified time period. If the form is not returned, the corporation will be forfeited. This means that the corporation will cease to exist as a legal entity. This happens all the time. Worse, it is always discovered at a critical time — usually when the lawsuit has arrived and the pastor is being sued personally because no corporation exists or just before you are about to close on a building loan.

The point is a simple one. Someone needs to make sure this information stays up to date.

Article 9
Board of Directors

All non-profit corporations are required to have a board of directors. Just as with for-profit companies, the board is responsible for running the corporation and making major decisions. Accordingly, the board members should be people that you trust and respect. In addition, board members should be able to add value to the organization.

In most states, you are required to name a minimum of three (3) board members and you can have as many directors as you like. However, to avoid the potential for stalemates, you should avoid having an even number of people on the board (a four person board can be divided two against two). In addition, large boards become cumbersome (it can be difficult to set-up meetings) and hard to manage (increasing the board size increases the potential for having board members with different personal agendas, etc.). I suggest creating a board of three or five members at the outset.

As will be discussed later, the board is either the most powerful entity in your corporate structure or the second most powerful. In some cases, the church membership is empowered to elect the board members and, as a result, the membership retains ultimate power under such a structure. In other cases, the corporation is structured so that the board elects itself or is appointed by an individual or committee. In these cases, the board is the most powerful entity in the corporation.

Choosing a good board is vital to the long-term success of your corporation. A board of yes men will provide no real assistance or guidance. On the other hand, a renegade board can cause division. You need smart, serious people who can add value to your ministry.

Article 10

Limitation of Liability of Directors

This provision is very important to you and anyone else who chooses to serve on your board. This simple statement means that a board member is only liable to the corporation for those acts mandated by law. Most states allow a corporation to agree, in its Articles of Incorporation, to relieve its board members of liability to the corporation for any acts, unless those acts violate the board members duties of loyalty and good faith and fair dealing to the corporation.

Because of this, all board members need to understand these concepts. Boiled down, a board member has an obligation to act in good faith to do what is best for the corporation. The board member cannot put his or her own interest above that of the corporation. It also means that the board member has an obligation to TRY to do the right thing. There is no obligation that the board member be right 100% of the time, only an obligation to try.

In the real world this means that the board member needs to regularly attend meetings, attempt to be informed about the decisions that are being made and not act out of self-interest.

Here is an example of how this works. Deacon Wilson is one of your board members and is in the real estate business. The church needs property for a new building. Deacon Wilson is placed in charge of the search and it is his duty to find the best deal for the church. Deacon Wilson reports back that a certain property is the only one that works and it is available for only $1,000,000. But he fails to tell the rest of the board that he owns that property, that it is only worth $500,000 and that 5 other cheaper and better properties exist. In this case, Deacon Wilson has violated his duty of loyalty and good faith to the corporation and the corporation can sue him if they found out this information after they acted on his recommendation.

It is worth noting that if Deacon Wilson's property really is the best choice, it is OK for the church to buy it as long as the deal is fair and after disclosing his interest, he does not vote on the decision. Remember that Deacon Wilson cannot use the corporation for his own self-interest or benefit.

Article 11

Indemnification

Well-drafted Articles will contain a provision stating that the corporation will indemnify its officers and directors for actions taken in the course of their official duties. This provision provides critical protection for the individuals who run the church. Very often when a church, as a corporation, is sued for some alleged misconduct (for instance, a former employee sues alleging sexual harassment), the individual board members of the church may also be sued (usually based on some idea that the individual allowed the wrong to occur). When that happens, you, as an individual who has been sued, will need to obtain counsel to defend yourself and your interests (your interests may or may not differ from the interests of the church) and that will cost money. If the Articles (or Bylaws) have been drafted properly, you will be able to look to the church for protection.

By agreeing in the Articles (or bylaws) to indemnify its officer or directors, the church is saying that it will defend you in case you are sued as a result of your official acts. This means the church will hire a lawyer to represent you and also pay any judgment if you lose that lawsuit.

One important note here, just because a church has agreed in the Articles to indemnify its officers and directors, it does not guarantee that the church will have the capacity to follow-through on that promise. Accordingly, you need to insist that your church obtain Directors and Officers insurance as part of its standard insurance package. This coverage will provide the funding to allow the church to meet its commitments in the event that its officer or directors are sued.

In addition, this indemnity will not extend to acts that violate the duty of good faith or loyalty. At the point in time that the corporation determines that the director in question violated his duty to the corporation, the corporation may drop its defense.

Article 12

Construction

This is simply a legal notation that means that your Articles will be interpreted in light of the then current version of your states non-profit corporation law. By having this provision, you avoid having to re-draft your Articles every time corporate laws change.

Article 13

Incorporators

This section lists the person(s) who sign and file the Articles of Incorporation. Typically, this is the lawyer who prepared and filed the document.

Article 14

Action by Written Consent

By allowing your corporation to act by consent, you will save yourself a lot of time and trouble. Very simply, this means that when the board agrees on a course of action, the members can all sign a written statement to that effect (which can be done by fax) and there is no need to convene a formal meeting.

Bylaws

At the same time the Articles of Incorporation are prepared, your lawyer will need to prepare bylaws for the corporation. Together with the Articles of Incorporation, the bylaws form the governing documents of the corporation. In essence, the bylaws set forth the rules for operating the corporation. As I always tell my clients, the bylaws are meaningless until you have a dispute about some course of action the church is going to take, then the bylaws become all important. The bylaws will set forth all of the formal rules that a corporation needs to follow to implement an official course of action.

As a pastor, you need to review your bylaws with an eye to what would occur in the event of a split in your church. If two groups want to move in disparate directions, the bylaws will inevitably dictate who will win the battle and the war. The bylaws accomplish this by setting out who has the power to take a specific action.

For example, I know of a church split that occurred between a new, young pastor and a board controlled by the allies of the recently retired pastor and church founder. As sometimes happens, the retired pastor was not really ready to let go and he used his allies on the board to drive out the young pastor. Despite the ability and popularity of the young pastor, this war was over before it ever started because the Articles of Incorporation and bylaws of the church gave the small board ultimate authority over the pastor and the will of the congregation. The young pastor's only option was to leave and start a new church. If you take over a situation, learn what the ground rules are. Without this knowledge, you are unprepared to act.

Before proceeding, a quick word on the organizational structure of corporations may be beneficial. With a for-profit corporation, whether it is General Motors or Al's Burger Barn, there are three layers of power. Ultimate power always resides with the shareholders of the corporation. The shareholders own the company and ultimately call the shots. In turn, the shareholders elect the Board of Directors of the Corporation. The Board is the policy and direction setting body of the corporation. Because it is a smaller group, the board meets on a regular basis to oversee the operations of the business. In turn, the Board is charged with electing the officers of the corp. The officers are the actual people charged with running the day-to-day operations of the business. The officers include the President. Vice Presidents (if any), Secretary, and Treasurer. These people may or may not be board members or shareholders.

With Al's Burger Barn, Al may be the sole shareholder, the Chairman of the Board and the President. Larger companies such as GM delegate power to the board and officers. In a company such as GM that has tens of thousands of shareholders, the board runs the company. However, if enough of the shareholders do not like the way things are being run, they can get together at the annual meeting and replace the management.

Structure of a For-Profit Corporation

SHAREHOLDERS
- own the corporation
- elect board of directors

↓

BOARD OF DIRECTORS
- set corporate policy and make major decisions
- elect the officers

↓

OFFICERS (PRESIDENT, VICE PRESIDENT, ETC.)
- responsible for operation of company

With a non-profit corporation, the set-up is a little different. There are no owners. A non-profit and its assets do not belong to any individuals. Therefore, there is no preset ultimate authority equivalent to shareholders. However, a non-profit corporation still must rely upon people to run it. Like a for-profit company, a non-profit corporation will have a Board of Directors and officers (with functions similar to their counterparts in a for-profit company). A church, unlike a for-profit corporation, does not have owners and, therefore, has no shareholders. A church, however, typically has members. Those members, while they have no ownership stake, may or may not have a say in how the church is run. It is the organizational documents of the church (the articles and bylaws) that set forth exactly how power is divided among the members, the board and the officers.

In most states, the law grants broad authority for individual non-profit corporations to draft bylaws that match its situation and needs. Therefore, bylaws can be custom tailored to any given situation. For the most part, however, the organizational structure of churches falls into three broad categories. First is the traditional congregation driven church. This is the structure used by many southern Baptist churches and other denominational structures. Under this structure, the church congregation is the highest decision making body in the church. The congregation is empowered to vote to make most major decisions and can hire and remove employees of the church up to and including removal of the pastor.

Next is the board driven church. In this type of organization, a relatively small board of directors (sometimes called trustees) has full authority to direct all activities of the church. While the church has members, those members are not granted any actual authority to govern the organization. The members cannot vote to remove a pastor or buy a new building.

The board driven structure can be modified to grant almost complete control to a single individual. For instance, a pastor can be granted perpetual office and the power to remove that pastor can be virtually eliminated. For instance, giving the pastor the right to remove and appoint the other board members gives the pastor unlimited corporate power because he or she can simply replace anyone who is hostile to the pastor.

Structure of a Board Driven Church

BOARD OF DIRECTORS

- elects itself or is appointed by designated individual
  elects officers

OFFICERS

- run the church

A word to the wise here, you need to maintain some independence among your board to address topics such as executive compensation. As will be discussed later, highly compensated pastors need an independent compensation committee to give them the protection that they need when dealing with tax matters. The point is that ultimately you need your lawyer to prepare balanced bylaws to look to the big picture and do not get obsessed with preventing an overthrow. The pastor's real authority is moral, not legal authority.

Third model is the hybrid structure. With a hybrid church, the members retain ultimate power on a few specific issues. For example, it is common for a hybrid structure church to have members that vote only to (i) elect a board of directors of the church who govern the day-to-day operations, (ii) remove and/or hire a pastor (usually requires a super majority of 75-80%, (iii) take on indebtedness to purchase property, or (iv) amend the bylaws. You can see that in such a structure, the board and staff have the authority to run day-to-day operations, but the members retain the ultimate controls. Most important is the power to amend the bylaws which gives the power to change the rules when it suits you.

Structure of a Hybrid Church

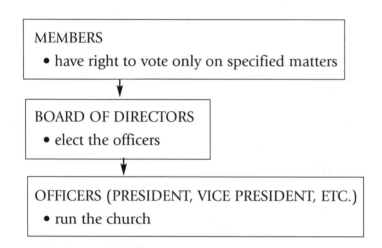

MEMBERS
- have right to vote only on specified matters

BOARD OF DIRECTORS
- elect the officers

OFFICERS (PRESIDENT, VICE PRESIDENT, ETC.)
- run the church

To help evaluate your bylaws, the following is a sample bylaws with options noted for different structures.

BYLAWS OF GLOBAL MEGA CHURCH, INC.

These Bylaws (the "Bylaws") govern the affairs of GLOBAL MEGA CHURCH, INC., a non-profit corporation (the

Corporation") organized under the Texas Non-Profit Corporation
Act, as amended (the "Act").

ARTICLE 1

OFFICES

Principal Office

1.01.The principal office of the Corporation shall be located at
_____. The office of the Corporation in the State of Texas
shall be located in _____, Texas. The Corporation may
have such other offices, as the Board of Directors may determine.
The Board of Directors may change the location of any office of the
Corporation.

Registered Office and Registered Agent

1.02.The Corporation shall comply with the requirements of
the Act and maintain a registered office and registered agent in
Texas. The registered office may, but need not, be identical with
the Corporation's principal office in Texas. The Board of Directors
may change the registered office and the registered agent as provided in the Act.

ARTICLE 2

NO MEMBERS

The Corporation shall not have members. The management of
the Corporation is vested solely in its Board of Directors.

[THIS SECTION WOULD BE MODIFIED, IF NEEDED TO PRO-
VIDE FOR MEMBERS AND THEIR POWERS]

ARTICLE 3

BOARD OF DIRECTORS

Management of the Corporation

The affairs of the Corporation shall be managed by the Board
of Directors.

Number, Qualifications and Tenure of Directors

3.02.The number of Directors shall be a number determined by
the Board of Directors that is not less than three and not greater
than nine. Directors need not be residents of any particular state.
Each director shall serve for a term of one year.

Election of Directors

3.03.Directors shall be elected, annually, by the Board of
Directors. Each director shall hold office until a successor is elected
and qualified. A director may be elected to succeed himself or herself
as director.

[OPTION: The Senior Pastor shall be a board member for life.
Board members shall be elected from those qualified individuals
nominated by the Senior Pastor].

Vacancies

3.04.Any vacancy occurring in the Board of Directors, and any
director position to be filled due to an increase in the number of
directors, shall be filled by the President. A director appointed to

fill a vacancy shall be appointed for the remainder of the term of the predecessor in office.

Annual Meeting

The annual meeting of the Board of Directors shall be held in a place and at a time determined by Board of Directors.

Regular Meetings

The Board of Directors may provide for regular meetings by resolution stating the time and place of such meetings. The meetings may be held at the place designated by the Board of Directors and shall be held at the Corporation's principal office if the resolution does not specify the location of the meetings. No notice of regular meetings of the Board is required other than a resolution of the Board of Directors stating the time and place of the meetings.

Special Meetings

Special meetings of the Board of Directors may be called by or at the request of the President or any two directors. A person or persons authorized to call special meetings of the Board of Directors may fix any place as the place for holding a special meeting. The person or persons calling a special meeting shall notify the secretary of the information required to be included in the notice of the meeting. The secretary shall give notice to the directors as required in the Bylaws.

Notice

Written or printed notice of any special meeting of the Board of Directorsshall be delivered to each director not less than three nor more than thirty days before the date of the meeting. The notice shall state the place, day, and time of the meeting, who called the meeting, and the purpose or purposes for which the meeting is called.

Quorum

A majority of the number of directors then in office shall constitute a quorumfor the transaction of business at any meeting of the Board of Directors. The directors present at a duly called or held meeting at which a quorum is present may continue to transact business even if enough directors leave the meeting so that less than a quorum remains. However, no action may be approved without the vote of at least a majority of the number of directors required to constitute a quorum. If a quorum is present at no time during a meeting, a majority of the directors present may adjourn and reconvene the meeting one time without further notice.

Duties of Directors

3.10.Directors shall discharge their duties, including any duties as committee members, in good faith, with ordinary care, and in a manner they reasonably believe to be in the best interest of the corporation. Ordinary care is care that ordinarily prudent persons in similar positions would exercise under similar circumstances. In the discharge of any duty imposed or power conferred on directors, they may in good faith rely on information, opinions, reports, or statements, including financial statements and other financial data, concerning the Corporation or another person that were prepared or presented by a variety of persons, including officers and employees of the Corporation, professional advisors or experts such as accountants or legal counsel. A director is not relying in good faith if the director has knowledge concerning a matter in question that renders reliance unwarranted.

Directors are not deemed to have the duties of trustees of a trust with respect to the Corporation or with respect to any property held or administered by the Corporation, including property that may be subject to restrictions imposed by the donor or transferor of the property.

Delegation of Duties

Directors are entitled to select advisors and delegate duties and responsibilities to them, such as the full power and authority to purchase or otherwise acquire stocks, bonds, securities, and other investments on behalf of the Corporation; and to sell, transfer, or otherwise dispose of the Corporation's assets and properties at a time and for a consideration that the advisor deems appropriate. The directors have no liability for actions taken or omitted by the advisor if the Board of Directors acts in good faith and with ordinary care in selecting the advisor. The Board of Directors may remove or replace the advisor, with or without cause.Interested Directors

Contracts or transactions between directors, officers, or members who have afinancial interest in the matter are not void or voidable solely for that reason. Nor are they void or voidable solely because the director, officer, or member is present at or participates in the meeting that authorizes the contract or transaction, or solely because the interested party's votes are counted for the purpose. However, the material facts must be disclosed to or known by the board or other group authorizing the transaction, and adequate approval from disinterested parties must be obtained or the transaction must be fair to the Corporation.

Actions of Board of Directors

The Board of Directors shall try to act by consensus. However, the vote of amajority of directors present and voting at a meeting at which a quorum is present shall be sufficient to constitute the act of the Board of Directors unless the act of a greater number is required by law or the Bylaws. A director who is present at a meeting and abstains from a vote is considered to be present and voting for the purpose of determining the decision of the Board of Directors. For the purpose of determining the decision of the Board of Directors, a director who is represented by proxy in a vote is considered present.

Proxies

A director may vote by proxy executed in writing by the director. No proxyshall be valid after three (3) months from the date of its execution.

Compensation

Directors may not receive salaries for their services. The Board of Directors may adopt a resolution providing for payment to directors of the reasonable expenses of attendance, if any, for attendance at each meeting of the Board of Directors. A director may serve the Corporation in any other capacity and receive compensation for those services. Any compensation that the Corporation pays to a director shall be commensurate with the services performed and reasonable in amount.

Removal of Directors

A director may be removed at any time by a majority of the Board of Directors.

[OPTION: The Senior Pastor may remove a director at any

time.] This option grants ultimate power to the Senior Pastor because hostile directors can be removed.

ARTICLE 4

OFFICERS

Officer Positions

The officers of the Corporation shall be a president, a secretary, and may include any number of vice presidents, a treasurer, an assistant treasurer and an assistant secretary. The Board of Directors may create additional officer positions, define the authority and duties of each such position, and elect or appoint persons to fill the positions. Any two or more offices may be held by the same person, except the offices of president and secretary.

Election and Term of Office

4.02. The officers of the Corporation shall be elected annually by the Board of Directors at the regular annual meeting of the Board of Directors. If the election of officers is not held at this meeting, the election shall be held as soon thereafter as conveniently possible. Each officer shall hold office until a successor is duly selected and qualified. An officer may be elected to succeed himself or herself in the same office.

Removal

4.03. Any officer elected or appointed by the Board of Directors may be removed by the Board of Directors with or without good cause; provided, however, that the removal of the President shall require a unanimous vote of the Board of Directors. The removal of an officer shall be without prejudice to the contract rights, if any, of the officer.

NOTE: This means that the board cannot remove the President if the President is also on the board.

Vacancies

A vacancy in any office may be filled by the Board of Directors for the remainder of the portion of the officer's term.

President

4.05. The President shall be the chief executive officer of the Corporation. The President shall supervise and control all of the business and affairs of the Corporation. The President shall preside at all meetings of the members and of the Board of Directors. The President may execute any deeds, mortgages, bonds, contracts, or other instruments that the Board of Directors has authorized to be executed. The President shall perform other duties prescribed by the Board of Directors and all duties incident to the office of President.

NOTE: It is typical to also state that the Senior Pastor of the church shall be the President.

Vice President

When the President is absent, is unable to act, or refuses to act, a Vice President shall perform the duties of the President. When a Vice President acts in place of the President, the Vice President shall have all the powers of and be subject to all the restrictions upon the President. If there is more than one Vice President, the Vice Presidents shall act in place of the President in the order of the votes received when elected. A Vice President shall perform other duties as assigned by the President or board of directors.

Except as expressly authorized by the board of directors, the vice president of public relations shall have no authority to sign for or otherwise bind the Corporation.

Treasurer

4.07.The treasurer shall:

(a)Have charge and custody of, and be responsible for, all funds and securities of the Corporation.

(b)Receive and give receipts for moneys due and payable to the Corporation from any source.

(c) Deposit all moneys in the name of the Corporation in banks, trust companies, or other depositaries as provided in the bylaws or as directed by the Board of Directors or President.

(d)Write checks and disburse funds to discharge obligations of the Corporation.

(e)Maintain the financial books and records of the Corporation.

(f)Prepare financial reports at least annually.

(g)Perform other duties as assigned by the President or by the Board of Directors.

(h)If required by the Board of Directors, give a bond for the faithful discharge of his or her duties in a sum and with a surety as determined by the Board of Directors.

(i)Perform all of the duties incident to the office of treasurer.

Secretary

4.08.The Secretary shall:

(a)Give all notices as provided in the bylaws or as required by law.

(b)Take minutes of the meetings of the members and of the Board of Directors and keep the minutes as part of the corporate records.

(c)Maintain custody of the corporate records and of the seal of the Corporation.

(d)Affix the seal of the Corporation to all documents as authorized.

(e)Keep a register of the mailing address of each director, officer, and employee of the Corporation.

(f)Perform duties as assigned by the President or by the Board of Directors.

(g)Perform all duties incident to the office of secretary.

ARTICLE 5

COMMITTEES

Establishment of Committees

5.01.The Board of Directors may adopt a resolution establishing one or more committees delegating specified authority to a committee, and appointing or removing members of a committee. A committee shall include two or more directors and may include persons who are not directors. If the Board of Directors delegates any of its authority to a committee, the majority of the committee shall consist of directors. The Board of Directors may establish qualifications for membership on a committee. The Board of Directors may delegate to the President its power to appoint and remove members of a committee that has not been delegated any authority of the Board of Directors. The establishment of a committee or the delegation of authority to it shall not relieve the Board of Directors, or any individual director, of any responsibility imposed by the bylaws or otherwise imposed by law. No committee shall have the authority of the Board of Directors to:

(a)Amend the articles of incorporation.

(b)Adopt a plan of merger or a plan of consolidation with another Corporation.

(c)Authorize the sale, lease, exchange, or mortgage of all or substantially all of the property and assets of the Corporation.

(d)Authorize the voluntary dissolution of the Corporation.

(e)Revoke proceedings for the voluntary dissolution of the Corporation.

(f)Adopt a plan for the distribution of the assets of the Corporation.

(g)Amend, alter, or repeal the bylaws.

(h)Elect, appoint, or remove a member of a committee or a director or officer of the Corporation.

(i)Approve any transaction to which the Corporation is a party and that involves a potential conflict of interest as defined in paragraph 5.04, below.

(j)Take any action outside the scope of authority delegated to it by the Board of Directors.

Term of Office

5.02.Each member of a committee shall continue to serve on the committee until the next annual meeting of the members of the Corporation and until a successor is appointed. However, the term of a committee member may terminate earlier if the committee is terminated, or if the member dies, ceases to qualify, resigns, or is removed as a member. A vacancy on a committee may be filled by an appointment made in the same manner as an original appointment. A person appointed to fill a vacancy on a committee shall serve for the remainder of the portion of the terminated committee member's term.

Chair and Vice-Chair

5.03. One member of each committee shall be designated as the chair of the committee and another member of each committee shall be designated as the vice-chair. The chair and vice-chair shall be elected by the members of the committee. The chair shall call and preside at all meetings of the committee. When the chair is absent, is unable to act, or refuses to act, the vice-chair shall perform the duties of the chair. When a vice-chair acts in place of the chair, the vice-chair shall have all the powers of and be subject to all the restrictions upon the chair.

Notice of Meetings

5.04. Written or printed notice of a committee meeting shall be delivered to each member of a committee not less than seven (7) nor more than thirty (30) days before the date of the meeting. The notice shall state the place, day, and time of the meeting, and the purpose or purposes for which the meeting is called.

Quorum

5.05. One half the number of members of a committee shall constitute a quorum for the transaction of business at any meeting of the committee. The committee members present at a duly called or held meeting at which a quorum is present may continue to transact business even if enough committee members leave the meeting so that less than a quorum remains. However, no action may be approved without the vote of at least a majority of the number of committee members required to constitute a quorum. If a quorum is present at no time during a meeting, the chair may adjourn and reconvene the meeting one time without further notice.

Actions of Committees

5.06.Committees shall try to take action by consensus. However, the vote of a majority of committee members present and voting at a meeting at which a quorum is present shall be sufficient to constitute the act of the committee unless the act of a greater number is required by law or the bylaws. A committee member who is present at a meeting and abstains from a vote is considered to be present and voting for the purpose of determining the act of the committee.Proxies

5.07A committee member may vote by proxy executed in writing by the committee member. No proxy shall be valid after three months from the date of its execution.

Compensation

5.08.Committee members shall not receive salaries for their services. The Board of Directors may adopt a resolution providing for payment to committee members of the expenses of attendance, if any, for attendance at each meeting of the committee. A committee member may serve the Corporation in any other capacity and receive compensation for those services. Any compensation that the Corporation pays to a committee member shall be commensurate with the services performed and shall be reasonable in amount.

Rules

5.09.Each committee may adopt rules for its own operation not inconsistent with the bylaws or with rules adopted by the Board of Directors.

ARTICLE 6

TRANSACTIONS OF THE CORPORATION

Contracts

6.01.The Board of Directors may authorize any officer or agent of the Corporation to enter into a contract or execute and deliver any instrument in the name of and on behalf of the Corporation. This authority may be limited to a specific contract or instrument or it may extend to any number and type of possible contracts and instruments.

Deposits

6.02.All funds of the Corporation shall be deposited to the credit of the Corporation in banks, trust companies, or other depositaries that the Board of Directors selects.

Gifts

6.03.The Board of Directors may accept on behalf of the Corporation any contribution, gift, bequest, or devise for the general purposes or for any special purpose of the Corporation. The Board of Directors may make gifts and give charitable contributions that are not prohibited by the bylaws, the articles of incorporation, state law, and any requirements for maintaining the Corporation's federal and state tax status.

Potential Conflicts of Interest

6.04.The Corporation shall not make any loan to a director or officer of the Corporation. A director, officer, or committee member of the Corporation may lend money to and otherwise transact business with the Corporation except as otherwise provided by the bylaws, articles of incorporation, and all applicable laws. Such a person transacting business with the Corporation has the same rights and obligations relating to those matters as other persons transacting business with the Corporation. The Corporation shall not borrow money from or otherwise transact business with a director, officer, or committee member of the Corporation unless the transaction is described fully in a legally binding instrument and is in the best interests of the Corporation. The Corporation shall not borrow money from or otherwise transact business with a director, officer, or committee member of the Corporation without full disclosure of all relevant facts and without the approval of the Board of Directors, not including the vote of any person having a personal interest in the transaction.

Prohibited Acts

6.05.As long as the Corporation is in existence, and except with the prior approval of the Board of Directors, no director, officer, or committee member of the Corporation shall:

(a)Do any act in violation of the bylaws or a binding obligation of the Corporation.

(b)Do any act with the intention of harming the Corporation or any of its operations.

(c)Do any act that would make it impossible or unnecessarily difficult to carry on the intended or ordinary business of the Corporation.

(d)Receive an improper personal benefit from the operation of the Corporation.

(e)Use the assets of this Corporation, directly or indirectly, for any purpose other than carrying on the business of this Corporation.

(f)Wrongfully transfer or dispose of Corporation property, including intangible property such as good will.

(g)Use the name of the Corporation (or any substantially similar name) or any trademark or trade name adopted by the Corporation, except on behalf of the Corporation in the ordinary course of the Corporation's business.

(h)Disclose any of the Corporation business practices, trade secrets, or any other information not generally known to the business community to any person not authorized to receive it.

ARTICLE 7

BOOKS AND RECORDS

Required Books and Records

7.01.The Corporation shall keep correct and complete books and records of account. The Corporation's books and records shall include:

(a)A file-endorsed copy of all documents filed with the Texas Secretary of State relating to the Corporation, including, but not limited to, the articles of incorporation, and any articles of amendment, restated articles, articles of merger, articles of consolidation, and statement of change of registered office or registered agent.

(b)A copy of the bylaws, and any amended versions or amendments to the bylaws.

(c)Minutes of the proceedings of the Board of Directors, and committees having any of the authority of the Board of Directors.

(d)A list of the names and addresses of the directors, officers, and any committee members of the Corporation.

(e)If prepared, a financial statement showing the assets, liabilities, and net worth of the Corporation at the end of the three most recent fiscal years.

(f)If prepared, a financial statement showing the income and expenses of the Corporation for the three most recent fiscal years.

(g)All rulings, letters, and other documents relating to the Corporation's federal, state, and local tax status.

Inspection and Copying

7.02.Any director, officer, or member of the Corporation may inspect and receive copies of all books and records of the Corporation required to be kept by the bylaws. Such a person may inspect or receive copies if the person has a proper purpose related to the person's interest in the Corporation and if the person submits a request in writing. Any person entitled to inspect and copy the Corporation's books and records may do so through his or her attorney or other duly authorized representative. A person entitled to inspect the Corporation's books and records may do so at a reasonable time no later than five working days after the Corporation's receipt of a proper written request. The Board of Directors may establish reasonable fees for copying the Corporation's books and records by members. The fees may cover the cost of materials and labor, but may not exceed fifty cents per page. The Corporation shall provide requested copies of books or records no later than five working days after the Corporation's receipt of a proper written request.

ARTICLE 8

FISCAL YEAR

The fiscal year of the Corporation shall begin on the first day of January and end on the last day in December in each year.

ARTICLE 9

INDEMNIFICATION

When Indemnification is Required, Permitted, and Prohibited

9.01.To the greatest extent permitted by the Act, the Corporation shall indemnify a director, officer, committee member, employee, or agent of the Corporation who was, is, or may be named defendant or respondent in any proceeding as a result of his or her actions or omissions within the scope of his or her official capacity in the Corporation.

Procedures Relating to Indemnification Payments

9.02.(a)Before the Corporation may pay any indemnification expenses (including attorney's fees), the Corporation shall specifically determine that indemnification is permissible, authorize indemnification, and determine that expenses to be reimbursed are reasonable. The Corporation may make these determinations and decisions by any one of the following procedures:

(i) Majority vote of a quorum consisting of directors who, at the time of the vote, are not named defendants or respondents in the proceeding.

(ii) If such a quorum cannot be obtained, by a majority vote of a committee of the Board of Directors, designated to act in the matter by a majority vote of all directors, consisting solely of two or more directors who at the time of the vote are not named defendants or respondents in the proceeding.

(iii) Determination by special legal counsel selected by the
Board of Directors by vote as provided in paragraph 9.02(a)(i) or
9.02(a)(ii), or if such a quorum cannot be obtained and such a
committee cannot be established, by a majority vote of all directors.

(b)The Corporation shall authorize indemnification and determine that expenses to be reimbursed are reasonable in the same
manner that it determines whether indemnification is permissible.
If the determination that indemnification is permissible is made by
special legal counsel, authorization of indemnification and determination of reasonableness of expenses shall be made in the manner specified by paragraph 9.02(a)(iii) above, governing the selection of special legal counsel. A provision contained in the articles
of incorporation, the bylaws, or a resolution of members or the
Board of Directors that requires the indemnification permitted by
paragraph 9.01 above, constitutes sufficient authorization of
indemnification even though the provision may not have been
adopted or authorized in the same manner as the determination
that indemnification is permissible.

(c)The Corporation shall pay indemnification expenses before
final disposition of a proceeding only after the Corporation determines that the facts then known would not preclude indemnification and the Corporation receives a written affirmation and undertaking from the person to be indemnified. The determination that
the facts then known to those making the determination would
not preclude indemnification and authorization of payment shall
be made in the same manner as a determination that indemnification is permissible under paragraph 9.02(a) above. The person's
written affirmation shall state that he or she has met the standard

of conduct necessary for indemnification under the bylaws. The written undertaking shall provide for repayment of the amount paid or reimbursed by the Corporation if it is ultimately determined that the person has not met the requirements for indemnification. The undertaking shall be an unlimited general obligation of the person, but it need not be secured and it may be accepted without reference to financial ability to make repayment.

ARTICLE 10

NOTICES

Notice by Mail or Telegram

10.01. Any notice required or permitted by the bylaws to be given to a director, officer, or member of a committee of the Corporation may be given by mail or telegram. If mailed, a notice shall be deemed to be delivered when deposited in the United States mail addressed to the person at his or her address as it appears on the records of the Corporation, with postage prepaid. If given by telegram, a notice shall be deemed to be delivered when accepted by the telegraph company and addressed to the person at his or her address as it appears on the records of the Corporation. A person may change his or her address by giving written notice to the secretary of the Corporation.

Signed Waiver of Notice

10.02. Whenever any notice is required to be given under the provisions of the Act or under the provisions of the articles of incorporation or the bylaws, a waiver in writing signed by a person entitled to receive a notice shall be deemed equivalent to the giving of the notice. A waiver of notice shall be effective whether signed before or after the time stated in the notice being waived.

Waiver of Notice by Attendance

10.03.The attendance of a person at a meeting shall constitute a waiver of notice of the meeting unless the person attends for the express purpose of objecting to the transaction of any business because the meeting is not lawfully called or convened.

ARTICLE 11

SPECIAL PROCEDURES CONCERNING MEETINGS

Meeting by Telephone

11.01.The Board of Directors, and any committee of the Corporation may hold a meeting by telephone conference-call procedures in which all persons participating in the meeting can hear each other. The notice of a meeting by telephone conference must state the fact that the meeting will be held by telephone as well as all other matters required to be included in the notice. Participation of a person in a conference-call meeting constitutes presence of that person at the meeting.

Decision Without Meeting

11.02.Any decision required or permitted to be made at a meeting of the Board of Directors, or any committee of the Corporation may be made without a meeting. A decision without a meeting may be made if a written consent to the decision is signed by all of the persons entitled to vote on the matter. The original signed consents shall be placed in the Corporation minute book and kept with the Corporation's records.

Voting by Proxy

11.03.A person who is authorized to exercise a proxy may not exercise the proxy unless the proxy is delivered to the officer presiding at the meeting before the business of the meeting begins. The secretary or other person taking the minutes of the meeting shall record in the minutes the name of the person who executed the proxy and the name of the person authorized to exercise the proxy. If a person who has duly executed a proxy personally attends a meeting, the proxy shall not be effective for that meeting. A proxy filed with the secretary or other designated officer shall remain in force and effect until the first of the following occurs:

(a)An instrument revoking the proxy is delivered to the secretary or other designated officer.

(b)The proxy authority expires under the terms of the proxy.

(c)The proxy authority expires under the terms of the Bylaws.

ARTICLE 12

AMENDMENTS TO BYLAWS

The bylaws may be altered, amended, or repealed, and new bylaws may be adopted by the Board of Directors. The notice of any meeting at which the bylaws are altered, amended, or repealed, or at which new bylaws are adopted shall include the text of the proposed bylaw provisions as well as the text of any existing provisions proposed to be altered, amended, or repealed. Alternatively, the notice may include a fair summary of those provisions.

ARTICLE 13

MISCELLANEOUS PROVISIONS

Legal Authorities Governing Construction of Bylaws

13.01.The bylaws shall be construed in accordance with the laws of the State of Texas. All references in the bylaws to statutes, regulations, or other sources of legal authority shall refer to the authorities cited, or their successors, as they may be amended from time to time.

Legal Construction

13.02.If any bylaw provision is held to be invalid, illegal, or unenforceable in any respect, the invalidity, illegality, or unenforceability shall not affect any other provision and the bylaws shall be construed as if the invalid, illegal, or unenforceable provision had not been included in the bylaws.

Headings

13.03.The headings used in the bylaws are used for convenience and shall not be considered in construing the terms of the bylaws.

Gender

13.04.Wherever the context requires, all words in the bylaws in the male gender shall be deemed to include the female or neuter gender, all singular words shall include the plural, and all plural words shall include the singular.

Seal

13.05.The Board of Directors may provide for a corporate seal.

Power of Attorney

13.06.A person may execute any instrument related to the Corporation by means of a power of attorney if an original executed copy of the power of attorney is provided to the secretary of the Corporation to be kept with the Corporation records.

Parties Bound

13.07.The bylaws shall be binding upon and inure to the benefit of the directors, officers, committee members, employees, and agents of the Corporation and their respective heirs, executors, administrators, legal representatives, successors, and assigns except as otherwise provided in the bylaws.

CERTIFICATE OF SECRETARY

I certify that I am the duly elected and acting secretary of the Corporation and that the foregoing Bylaws constitute the Bylaws of the Corporation. These Bylaws were duly adopted by the Unanimous Written Consent of the Board of Directors of the Corporation dated _____,

DATED: June _____, 1997.

By: _____

Name: _____

Title: _____

Before moving on, a couple of quick points should be made about Bylaws. First, under most state laws, any officer, director or member of a non-profit corporation is entitled to inspect its books and records. This means that most church members have the right to see all of the books and records of your church. However, if your structure places no power in the hands of your members, you can avoid this issue by providing, in your Bylaws, that the members of your church are not members of the corporation for the purposes of state law and those church members have none of the powers granted to members under state law.

Next, please note that Section 6.04 of the sample Bylaws provides that the corporation may not make a loan to its officers or directors. This section is included because it reflects the law of most states. Generally, all board members who approve such a loan are liable for its repayment until the debtor does in fact repay the loan.

Organizational Minutes

After Articles of Incorporation have been drafted and filed and the bylaws have been prepared, the third step in the organizational process to hold an organizational meeting of the board of directors. The board members named in the Articles of Incorporation need to have their first meeting to take care of a few housekeeping matters. Very often, this first meeting is done by written consent (all of the named directors sign a consent resolution). At this meeting, the following actions need to be taken:

The Articles and the Bylaws need to be approved and ratified.

A Minute Book for keeping the Articles, Bylaws and Minutes need to be approved.

The Board needs to elect the initial officers of the corporation. Most states require the corporation to elect at least a President and a Secretary. As a general matter, the President is charged with running the corporation. The Senior Pastor is typically named the President of the corporation. The Secretary is charged with maintaining corporate records. For a more detailed description of duties, see the sample bylaws above.

The following is a sample of a Written Consent that takes care of all of the matters that need to be addressed at the organizational meeting.

WRITTEN CONSENT

The undersigned, being all of the directors named in the Articles of Incorporation of Global Mega Church, Inc., a Texas Non-Profit Corporation (the "Corporation"), hereby, pursuant to the provisions of Article 9.10.B of the Texas Business Corporation Act, consents to and approves the following resolutions and each and every action effected thereby:

1. Articles of Incorporation.

RESOLVED, that the Articles of Incorporation that were submitted to, and reviewed by, the Board of Directors of the Corporation and that have been filed in the office of the Secretary of State of the State of Texas on   , are approved, accepted, ratified, and adopted as the Corporation's Articles of Incorporation.

FURTHER RESOLVED, that the Secretary of the Corporation is directed to insert the Articles of Incorporation and the Certificate of Incorporation issued by the Secretary of State of the State of

Texas in the minute book of the Corporation.

2. Bylaws.

RESOLVED, that the Bylaws for the regulation and management of the affairs of the Corporation that were submitted to, and reviewed by, the Board of Directors of the Corporation are approved and adopted for and as the Bylaws of the Corporation, and the Secretary of the Corporation is directed to insert a copy of the Bylaws in the minute book of the Corporation.

3. Minute Book.

RESOLVED, that (a) the minute book presented to the Board of Directors of the Corporation is approved and adopted, and the action of the Secretary in inserting in it the Articles of Incorporation, the Certificate of Incorporation, and the Bylaws is ratified and approved, and (b) the Secretary is hereby directed to authenticate the minute book, to retain custody of it, and to insert therein minutes of any meeting and of other proceedings (or written waivers and consents to any shareholder or director action) of the shareholders and/or directors of the Corporation and other appropriate records of the Corporation.

4. Corporate Seal.

RESOLVED, that the corporate seal, an impression of which appears on the margin of this Consent, is hereby approved and adopted as the form of seal of the Corporation, provided that the use of such seal shall not be required upon, and shall not affect the validity of, any instrument issued or executed by the Corporation.

5.Number of Directors.

RESOLVED, that until further action by the Board of Directors or the shareholders of the Corporation,   directors shall constitute the entire Board of Directors of the Corporation.

6. Election of Officers.

RESOLVED, that the following individuals are elected to the offices of the Corporation set forth opposite their respective names, each to serve as such until such officer's successor is elected or appointed and qualified or, if earlier, until such officer's death, resignation, or removal from office:

President

Secretary

7. Compensation of Officers.

RESOLVED, that until further action by the Board of Directors of the Corporation, the officers of the Corporation shall serve as such without salary or other compensation.

8. Banking and Borrowing.

RESOLVED, that the Corporation establish such banking arrangements as from time to time become necessary, desirable or appropriate, including arrangements with respect to establishing and maintaining checking accounts and with respect to borrowing funds, and that the signatures of all directors of the Corporation at the bottom of the form of certificate of resolution(s) customarily required by any such banking institution authorizing such arrangements shall constitute and be construed as a unanimous written consent to the adoption of such resolution(s) by the Board of Directors of the Corporation under the provisions of Article 9.10.B of the Texas Business Corporation Act, and that the Secretary of the Corporation is hereby authorized to certify to such resolution(s) so signed by all directors of the Corporation in such form as said banking institution may customarily require, and such resolution(s) so certified shall be deemed to be copied in the minute book as if set forth therein in full.

FURTHER RESOLVED, that the President and any other officer of the Corporation acting jointly are hereby authorized to borrow, from time to time, in the name and on behalf of the Corporation, such funds in such amounts from such persons or lending institutions as they, in their discretion, deem in the best interest of the Corporation.

FURTHER RESOLVED, that the signatures of all directors of the Corporation at the bottom of the form of certificate of resolution(s) customarily required by any such lenders authorizing such borrowing shall constitute and be construed as a unanimous written consent to the adoption of such resolution(s) by the Board of Directors of the Corporation under the provisions of Article 9.10.B of the Texas Business Corporation Act, and that the Secretary of the Corporation is hereby authorized to certify to such resolution(s) so signed by all directors of the Corporation in such form as said lender may customarily require, and such resolution(s) so certified shall be deemed to be copied in the minute book as if set forth therein in full.

9. Annual Meeting of Members.

RESOLVED, that the annual meeting of members of the Corporation shall be held during each calendar year on such date and at such time as shall be designated from time to time by the Board of Directors.

10. Organizational Expenses.

RESOLVED, that the appropriate officer of the Corporation be, and hereby is, authorized and directed to pay all charges and expenses incident to and necessary for the organization of the Corporation and to reimburse any person who has made any disbursement therefore.

11. Fiscal Year.

RESOLVED, that the fiscal year of the Corporation shall end on the last date of December each year.

12. Qualification to Transact Business as a Foreign Corporation.

RESOLVED, that the appropriate officers of the Corporation are hereby authorized and directed to cause the Corporation to qualify as a foreign corporation in such jurisdictions as may be legally required by reason of the property owned, business conducted, or other activities effected by the Corporation in such jurisdictions now or at any time hereafter.

13.Authorization.

RESOLVED, that the officers of the Corporation are hereby severally authorized (a) to sign, execute, certify to, verify, acknowledge, deliver, accept, file, and record any and all instruments and documents, and (b) to take, or cause to be taken, any and all such action, in the name and on behalf of the Corporation, as (in such officer's judgment) shall be necessary, desirable or appropriate in order to effect the purposes of the foregoing resolutions.

FURTHER RESOLVED, that any and all action taken by any proper officer of the Corporation prior to the date this [Unanimous] Consent is actually executed in effecting the purposes of the foregoing resolutions is hereby ratified, approved, confirmed, and adopted in all respects.

IN WITNESS WHEREOF, the undersigned directors of the Corporation have executed this Consent as of the date first above written.

_____

_____

A couple of quick points should be made about the Organizational Meeting. With regard to board membership, it is common for the board members of churches to serve without compensation. This is often a good idea and offers a distinct benefit. By serving without pay, board members are designated as "volunteers" and are afforded greater latitude by the courts. By this I mean that a court will not expect a volunteer board members to exercise as much diligence as a paid board member. In addition, some states offer limited legal protections for volunteers serving non-profit organizations.

The final step to forming your non-profit corporation is to apply for and receive your corporation's Employer Identification Number (EIN). This number is the equivalent of a social security number for a corporation. It is required to open a corporate bank account or conduct similar official business in the name of the corporation. Obtaining the number is a simple process. You simply complete a one-page form, call the IRS at the phone number designated for your state, give the IRS the information from the form and they will assign the number to you over the phone. Then you simply sign the form and mail it in to the IRS and you will receive a written confirmation in a few weeks.

At this point, you now have an official non-profit corporation. While this may appear to be time consuming and complex, it is really a simple process and can be completed literally within a day or two. The key is to have an understanding of the type of organizational structure that you want to have in place. If you are not sure, that is fine too. You can always amend your Articles of Incorporation or bylaws to implement a new structure (as long as all of the required parties agree).

Maintaining a Corporation

Now, all you have to do is maintain the existence of the corporation. As a general matter, maintaining a non-profit corporation is an easy matter. The basic steps are as follows:

Your Board (and your members if they have power in your corporation) needs to meet at least one time per year. At this meeting, board members need to be elected or re-elected, officers need to be elected, and you need to ratify all actions taken in the last year.

Your Board needs to approve all major actions of the corporation. Generally, any large purchase or borrowing of money should be approved by the Board.

You need to act as if you are operating a corporation. This means:

The corporation must have its own books and records.

All corporate expenses should be paid from the corporate account and corporate receipts should be paid into the corporate account.

All agreements should be signed in the name of the corporation. Do not sign corporate agreements unless the agreement names the corporation as the party to the contract.

Promptly file any forms required by your state. For instance, Texas requires non-profit corporations to file a Public Information Report listing its officers and directors. If you fail to file the form, your status as a corporation will be lost. Make sure that you respond to any notices from the state.

If you follow these simple rules, your corporate status should stay intact and offer you the intended protection.

Board Members

Prior to concluding this chapter, a quick word on the duty and obligation of board members is in order. Very often, potential board members have a concern for their personal liability. As a result, they decline to serve and the church is denied the benefit of their knowledge because they fear the unknown. In a properly structured corporation, board members have very little to fear. As long as the corporation organizational documents provide for indemnification of officers and directors as set forth above and the corporation carries director's and officer's insurance, the individual directors will be protected from most liability for their official acts.

As a general matter, the only time a director will not be covered is the occasion when a corporation cannot offer protection. That is when a director has violated his or her duty of loyalty and good faith to the corporation. A director has a duty to act in good faith in a manner that the director reasonably believes to be in the best interest of the corporation. This basically means that the director has a duty to try to do what he or she believes is best for the corporation. This does not mean that the director has to make the right decisions all the time (no one can). It only means that the director has to try to make the right decisions.

The most common example of a director violating this duty of loyalty and good faith is when a director engages in undisclosed self-dealing. By following a course of action that he or she knows is wrong and continuing despite the knowledge that the act is wrong or illegal is clearly a violation of his or her duty as a board member. Generally, there is no prohibition against a member of your board of directors engaging in a business transaction with your church (subject to the intermediate sanction rules listed in Chapter 2). However, two simple rules need to be met. First, the board members interest in the transaction should be disclosed to the full board and approved by a majority of the other board members (the involved board member should not vote on the item). Secondly, the transaction should be fair to the corporation.

One final note, board members need to make an effort to be right. This means attending meetings on a regular basis, gathering information and making a decision. Generally, board members are protected if they rely on information provided by officers of the corporation and the corporation's attorneys and accountants, unless they have reason to know that the information provided is false or if they know the person providing the information is unqualified to do so. As long as the information appears to be credible and from a credible source, board members may rely upon the data in making decisions.

Similar rules apply to the officers of the church. Like board members they have a duty of good faith and loyalty to the corporation. As a result, they also have a duty to try to do the right thing. The bottom line is that as long as you reasonably believe that the action you are taking is in the best interest of the corporation, you will find protection under today's corporate laws.

Multiple Corporations

Sometimes, it is advisable for a church or ministry to form multiple corporations because of the nature of their activities. Basically, the time and expense of forming additional corporations is worth it in two cases. First, when a church engages in high-risk activities, consideration should be given to isolating these activities in a stand-alone corporation. The purpose of this would be to protect the assets of the main church corporation in the event that the corporation housing the high-risk activities is sued and found liable for damages in an amount greater than the available insurance.

A common example is a school. Because schools involve the oversight of large numbers of young children, there is always the chance of liability. What happens if a teacher, for example, sexually assaults a student and the school is found liable for $10,000,000 in damages but only has $5,000,000 in available insurance. If a stand-alone corporation operates the school, only the assets of that corporation are subject to being seized to pay the judgment. However, if the church operates the school through the same corporation as the church, then the assets of the church are subject to the judgment.

One note here, in some states non-profit corporations are given special protections from many types of lawsuits. If you are in one of those states, such as Texas, your lawyer can take those available protections into account when trying to help you evaluate the risk level of your activities and whether a separate corporation is needed.

The other time a separate corporation is needed is when you want to engage in activities that would create liability for unrelated business income taxes. For instance, real estate investments by the church or other investments in businesses may create unrelated business income. In those cases, it is wise to isolate that income (and the need to pay taxes) in a corporation separate from the church. This will prevent the church from having to file a tax return (and consequently disclosing private financial information).

As a tool and resource for you, the following is a listing of the contact information for the Secretary of State's Office for each state. Generally, the Secretary of State in each state is responsible for accepting the corporate filings of corporations in that state. Among other things, the Secretary of State can tell you whether or not your corporation is currently in good standing in your state. Additionally, most questions that you have about filing requirements and fees can be answered by the Secretary of State's staff. You may also obtained copies of any documents that your corporation may have previously filed with the Secretary of State.

Offices of the Secretaries of State

STATE

ADDRESS

PHONE

Alabama

"http://www.sos.state.al.us" www.sos.state.al.us

PO Box 5616

334-242-5324

Montgomery, AL 36103-5616

Alaska

"http://www.gov.state.ak.us/ltgov" www.gov.state.ak.us/ltgov

PO Box 110015

907-465-3520

Juneau, AK 99811-0015

Arizona

"http://www.sosaz.com" www.sosaz.com

14 North 18th Ave

602-542-4285

Phoenix, AZ 85007

Arkansas

"http://www.sosweb.state.ar.us" www.sosweb.state.ar.us

501 Woodlane, Suite 310

501-682-3409

Little Rock, AR 72201-1023

California

"http://www.ss.ca.gov" www.ss.ca.gov

1500 11th Street

916-653-6814

Sacramento, CA 95814

Colorado

"http://www.sos.state.co.us" www.sos.state.co.us

1560 Broadway, Suite 200

303-894-2200

Denver, CO 80202

Connecticut

"http://www.sots.state.ct.us" www.sots.state.ct.us

30 Trinity Street

860-509-6212

Hartford, CT 06106

Delaware

"http://www.state.de.us/sos" www.state.de.us/sos

401 Federal Street, Suite 3

302-439-4111

Dover, DE 19901

Washington, DC

"http://www.dcboee.org" www.dcboee.org

441 Fourth Street, NW

Suite 250 N

202-727-2525

Washington, DC 20001

Florida

"http://www.dos.state.fl.us" www.dos.state.fl.us

PL-02, The Capitol

850-245-6500

Tallahassee, FL 32399-0250

Georgia

"http://www.sos.state.ga.us" www.sos.state.ga.us

214 State Capitol

404-656-2881

Atlanta, GA 30334

Hawaii

"http://www.hawaii.gov/icsd/test2.htm"
www.hawaii.gov/icsd/test2.htm

802 Lehua Ave.

Pearl City, HI 96782

Idaho

"http://www.idsos.state.id.us" www.idsos.state.id.us

700 W. Jefferson. Room 203

208-334-2300

PO Box 83720

Boise, ID 83720-0080

Illinois

"http://www.sos.state.il.us" www.sos.state.il.us

213 State Capitol

800-252-8980

Springfield, IL 62706

Indiana

"http://www.in.gov/sos" www.in.gov/sos

302 W. Washington, Room E-018

317-232-6576

Indianapolis, IN 46204

Iowa

"http://www.sos.state.ia.us" www.sos.state.ia.us

Iowa Secretary of StateóStatehouse

515-281-8993

Des Moines, IA 50319

Kansas

"http://www.kssos.org" www.kssos.org

Memorial Hall

785-296-4564

120 SW 10th Ave.

Topeka, KS 66612-1594

Kentucky

"http://www.sos.state.ky.us" www.sos.state.ky.us

700 Capitol Ave., Suite 152

502-564-3490

State Capitol

Frankfort, KY 40601

Louisiana

PO Box 94125

225-922-1000

"http://www.sec.state.la.us" www.sec.state.la.us

Baton Rouge, LA 70804-9125

Maine

"http://www.state.me.us/sos" www.state.me.us/sos

148 State House Station

207-626-8400

Augusta, ME 04333*Maryland*

"http://www.sos.state.md.us" www.sos.state.md.us

State House

410-974-5521

Annapolis, MD 21401

Massachusetts

"http://www.state.ma.us/sec" www.state.ma.us/sec

State House, Room 337

617-727-7030

Boston, MA 02133

Michigan

"http://www.sos.state.mi.us" www.sos.state.mi.us

(There is no "main" office—you have to contact the specific office for a specific county)

Minnesota

"http://www.state.mn.us/ebranch/sos"
www.state.mn.us/ebranch/sos

180 State Office Building

800-627-3529

100 Constitution Ave.

St. Paul, MN 55155-1299

Mississippi

"http://www.sos.state.ms.us" www.sos.state.ms.us

PO Box 136

601-359-1350

Jackson, MS 39205-0136

Missouri

"http://mosl.sos.state.mo.us/" http://mosl.sos.state.mo.us/

600 W. Main

573-751-4936

Jefferson, MS 65102

Montana

"http://sos.state.mt.us/css/index/asp"
http://sos.state.mt.us/css/index/asp

Room 260, Capitol

406-444-2034

PO Box 202801

Helena, MT 59620-2801

Nebraska

"http://www.nol.org/home/SOS" www.nol.org/home/SOS

Suite 2300, State Capitols

402-471-2554

Lincoln, NE 68509

Nevada

"http://sos.state.nv.us/" http://sos.state.nv.us/

101 N. Carson St.

775-684-5708

Carson City, NV 89701

New Hampshire

"http://webster.state.nh.us/sos" http://webster.state.nh.us/sos

State House, Room 204

603-271-3242

Concord, NH 03301

New Jersey

"http://www.state.nj.us/state" www.state.nj.us/state

PO Box 300

609-984-1900

Trenton, NJ 08625-0300

New Mexico

"http://www.sos.state.nm.us" www.sos.state.nm.us

State Capitol North Annex

Suite 300

505-827-3600

Santa Fe, NM 87503

New York

"http://www.dos.state.ny.us" www.dos.state.ny.us

123 William St.

212-417-5800

New York, NY 10038-3804

North Carolina

"http://www.secstate.nc.us" www.secstate.nc.us

PO Box 29622

Raleigh, NC 27626-0622

North Dakota

"http://www.state.nd.us/sec" www.state.nd.us/sec

600 E. Boulevard Ave.

Dept. 108

701-328-2900

Bismarck, ND 58505-0500*Ohio*

"http://www.state.oh.us/sos" www.state.oh.us/sos

180 E. Broad St., 16th Floor

Columbus, OH 43215

Oklahoma

http://www.sos.state.ok.us" www.sos.state.ok.us

2300 N. Lincoln Blvd., Room 101

405-522-4560

Oklahoma City, OK 73105-4897

Oregon

"http://www.sos.state.or.us" www.sos.state.or.us

State Capitol Building, Suite 141

Salem, OR 97310

Pennsylvania

"http://www.dos.state.pa.us" www.dos.state.pa.us

302 North Office Building

717-787-6458

Harrisburg, PA 17120

Rhode Island

"http://www.state.ri.us" www.state.ri.us

State House, Room 217

401-222-2357

Providence, RI 02903

South Carolina

"http://www.scsos.com" www.scsos.com

Edgar Brown Bldg.

803-734-2170

1205 Pendleton St., Suite 525

Columbia, SC 29201

South Dakota

"http://www.state.sd.us/sos/sos/htm"
www.state.sd.us/sos/sos/htm

Capitol Building

605-773-4845

500 E. Capitol Ave., Suite 204

Pierre, SD 57501-5070

Tennessee

"http://www.state.tn.us/sos" www.state.tn.us/sos

312 Eighth Avenue North

615-741-2078

6th Floor

Nashville, TN 37243

Texas

"http://www.sos.state.tx.us" www.sos.state.tx.us

1019 Brazos

512-463-5770

Room 1E.8

Austin, TX 78701

Utah

"http://www.commerce.state.ut.us" www.commerce.state.ut.us

160 East 300 South

801-530-4849

2nd Floor

Salt Lake City, UT 84114*Vermont*

"http://www.sec.state.vt.us" www.sec.state.vt.us

Redstone Building

802-828-2363

26 Terrace St., Drawer 9

Montpelier, VT 05609-1101

Virginia

"http://www.soc.state.va.us" www.soc.state.va.us

830 East Main Street, 14th Floor

804-786-2441

Richmond, VA 23219

Washington

"http://www.secstate.wa.gov" www.secstate.wa.gov

PO Box 40228

360-902-4151

Olympia, WA 98504-0228

West Virginia

"http://www.state.wv.us/sos" www.state.wv.us/sos

Bldg. 1, Suite 157-K

304-558-8000

1900 Kanawha Blvd. East

Charleston, WV 25305-0770

Wisconsin

"http://badger.state.wi.us/agencies/sos/"
http://badger.state.wi.us/agencies/sos/

30 W. Mifflin, 10th Floor

608-266-8888

Madison, WI 53702

Wyoming

"http://badger.state.wi.us/agencies/sos/"
http://badger.state.wi.us/agencies/sos/

State Capitol Building

307-777-7378

Cheyenne, WY 82002

CHAPTER TWO

GETTING AND MAINTAINING
TAX-EXEMPT STATUS

Thomas J. Winters

and

Dan Beirute

What is a non-profit and tax-exempt organization?

The words "non-profit" and "tax-exempt" are often used inter-changeably. However, the words describe two distinct legal concepts. The term "non-profit" describes an organization that is organized and operated for religious, charitable, scientific, or educational purposes. In order to be considered "non-profit," an organization needs only to file articles of incorporation as a non-profit corporation in the state in which it operates.

An organization that has filed its articles of incorporation to obtain non-profit status is not necessarily "tax-exempt." The term "tax-exempt" describes a non-profit organization that has been recognized by the Internal Revenue Service (IRS) as exempt from federal income taxes. Also, an organization that is exempt from federal income tax is not necessarily exempt from other types of taxes. For example, most churches are required by the federal government to withhold social security taxes from their employees' wages and to pay to the IRS a portion of the social security taxes attributable to the employees. States also may assess taxes, such as property taxes, sales taxes, or franchise taxes. In many cases, however, religious organizations are able to obtain exemption from some or all of these taxes, usually after filing an exemption application with the state.

How does a church maintain its non-profit status?

Sometimes while focusing on compliance with IRS rules, church leaders may forget the importance of complying with state government rules for maintaining a corporation's non-profit status. Failure to comply with these rules may result in the suspension of the corporation's "good standing" with the state. When a corporation lacks good standing with the state or when a corporation has been dissolved by the state as a result of the organization's failure to follow the rules discussed below, the trustees, officers, and even members of the organization may sometimes be held personally responsible for the debts and liabilities of the organization.

In order to maintain its good standing as a non-profit organization, a church should (a) update the state regarding the organization's registered agent and address; (b) domesticate into states in which the church maintains a regular operational presence; (c) amend its articles of incorporation or bylaws when needed to accurately reflect organizational changes; (d) conduct meetings of its board of trustees and record minutes of these meetings; and (e) file annual reports and charitable solicitations reports where required.

A. MAINTAIN ACCURATE REGISTERED AGENT AND ADDRESS

Church leaders should make sure that their state government maintains an accurate record of the registered address of the church. If a church moves, the church should inform the secretary of state of the state of incorporation of the new address. Churches should also take care to update the state regarding the name and address of the organization's registered agent. A registered agent is an individual charged with the duty of receiving official paperwork, such as notices from the state or lawsuits, on behalf of the corporation. If the name or address filed with the state for the registered agent is incorrect, a corporation may not even know that a lawsuit has been filed against it or if the state has attempted to forward the corporation a tax statement, refund, or corporate annual report form.

B. DOMESTICATE INTO NEW STATES OF OPERATION

Although non-profit organizations should update the state regarding address changes, additional requirements apply in the rare case of an organization moving into an entirely new state to conduct business. In that case, a church must "domesticate" into the new state. The process of domestication involves the filing of legal documents with the secretary of state of the new state, informing the state that the organization is beginning operations there. Non-profit organizations should domesticate into any state in which they are not incorporated but in which they have employees or operate an office or place of business. However, it is important to remember that domestication never relieves an organization from the duty of maintaining its non-profit status in the state of incorporation.

C. AMEND ARTICLES OF INCORPORATION

Occasionally, a church may need to amend its articles of incorporation, the document filed with the organization's state of incorporation to form the corporation. A church may need to amend its articles of incorporation to reflect a change in its governing structure, such as a change in the required number of members of the board of directors. A church may also amend its articles of incorporation in order to change its name. In order to replace an old name entirely, a church would file amended articles of incorporation with its state of incorporation, whereas a church merely intending to adopt an additional name without changing its original name would simply file a trade name (sometimes referred to as a "d/b/a") with the state or county.

D. CONDUCT MEETINGS OF TRUSTEES AND PREPARE MINUTES

Churches should conduct meetings of their board of trustees (also commonly referred to as "board of directors") at least annually. These meetings should typically be held at the beginning of the New Year or at the end of the year for the purposes of making decisions regarding the upcoming year. Meetings should focus on issues that the bylaws authorize the directors to decide. These issues typically include elections and termination of officers and directors, hiring or firing of key personnel, salary and housing allowance of ministers and key staff, decisions regarding the purchase of property or incurring of debt, and decisions regarding amendment of the bylaws or articles of incorporation.

The content of the meeting of directors should be recorded in written minutes. These minutes should be prepared as soon as possible following the meeting, to ensure that the minutes accurately reflect the content of the meeting and the decisions made at the meeting. Minutes should generally contain the names of the individuals attending the meeting, the date of the meeting, and a brief description of the decisions made at the meeting. In most cases, minutes do not need to describe issues which were discussed but not decided upon, and do not need to record the trustees' discussions in great detail. Brevity with accuracy should be the goal.

It is especially important for minutes to accurately record decisions regarding the approval of housing allowance for ministers, since ministers may receive housing allowance only after the allowance is properly authorized by the church.

E. AMEND BYLAWS

Church leaders should occasionally review their church bylaws to determine whether the bylaws require amendment to accurately reflect the church's governing style. State law requires corporations to act in accordance with the rules and guidelines set out under the corporate bylaws, so churches that do not adhere to the guidelines set out in the bylaws are technically acting illegally. Amendments to the bylaws should be approved by the congregation or board given the power of amendment under the set of bylaws being amended. For example, if the present set of bylaws calls for amendment by unanimous vote of the board of trustees, a unanimous vote is required, even if the amended set will call for a lesser number of trustees to approve future amendments. Amendments to bylaws are typically not filed with or issued to the state.

F. FILE CORPORATE ANNUAL REPORTS

A few states require churches to file corporate reports on an annual basis. The state usually sends the report form to the registered address of the organization required to file. These reports may require disclosure of information such as the names and addresses of corporate officers and trustees and the nature of the business conducted by the organization during the preceding year. Churches in states requiring filing of such reports should make sure to file the reports in a timely manner, since failure to file may result in revocation of corporate privileges.

G.FILE CHARITABLE SOLICITATIONS FILINGS

Another kind of filing which states are increasingly requiring of non-profit organizations is the charitable solicitation filing. Charitable solicitations laws, where applicable, require non-profit organizations soliciting donations in a state to file an initial registration application and an annual report thereafter. The registration and annual reports are filed with a state official—often the Attorney General—and frequently ask for the identity of the organization's officers and trustees, a description of the organization's operations, the amount of donations the organization has received, and the nature of the organization's fund raising efforts during the year.

To date, few states require ministries to file charitable solicitations reports, and even fewer states require churches to file. However, some state officials have recently called for greater state oversight and accountability over religious organizations, so churches may soon be required to make charitable solicitation filings in some states. Of course, churches should make sure to comply with the registration and annual filing requirements where they are applicable, in order to avoid the assessment of penalties or the revocation of corporate status.

How does a church obtain federal income tax exemption?

A.CHURCHES PRESUMED EXEMPT

Most non-profit corporations must file an application with the IRS requesting federal income tax exemption in order to be treated as exempt from federal income tax. Religious ministries, for example, must file the Form 1023, discussed below, before receiving approval for federal income tax exemption from the IRS. Churches, however, are technically presumed by the IRS to be exempt from federal income tax and therefore are not technically required to apply for recognition of exemption.

For churches, federal income tax exemption results automatically from operating as a "church" in the eyes of the IRS. As long as an organization meets the IRS definition of a church, the organization is considered exempt from federal income tax, even without filing an application for recognition of exemption. By contrast, religious organizations that do not qualify as churches, such as itinerant religious ministries, must file an application for recognition of exemption before being recognized as exempt from federal income taxation. In determining whether an organization qualifies as a church, the IRS considers a variety of facts and circumstances, including whether the organization has characteristics such as: (a) a recognized creed and form of worship; (b) an ecclesiastical government; (c) a formal code of doctrine and discipline; (d) ordained ministers; (e) an established place of worship; and (f) regular religious services.

B.JUSTIFICATION FOR APPLYING FOR EXEMPTION

Even though churches are technically not required to file for an application for exemption with the IRS, it is still a good idea to do so. Frequently, a church will be asked by its state or local government or by donors to provide evidence that the church is exempt from federal income tax. Churches that have filed for and obtained exemption will be listed in the IRS Publication 78, which lists the organizations recognized by the IRS as exempt, and will be able to provide an IRS "letter of determination," the IRS letter granting federal income tax exemption to the organization. Churches that have never filed for exemption are, of course, not listed in Publication 78 and are unable to provide a letter of determination. Although such churches are still exempt from federal income tax, it may be difficult and awkward for the church leaders to attempt to explain to a potential donor that the church is tax-exempt, or to explain to a state or city official that the church should be granted a property or sales tax exemption based upon the church's federal exemption, without documentation of exemption.

C. FILE FORM 1023

Churches wishing to apply for federal income tax exemption should retain an attorney to file the IRS Form 1023 with the Internal Revenue Service. The IRS charges a non-refundable $500.00 fee to process and review the form, although the fee may be reduced to $150.00 under certain circumstances when the church reports annual income of less than $10,000.00. The form is lengthy and requires disclosure of the identity of the organization's officers and trustees, a description of the organization's past and anticipated future activities, sources of financial support, intended fundraising programs, and statements of revenue and expense for the year of application and three previous years of operation, if any. Organizations in existence for less than three years must also provide budgets for the two years following the year of application. Along with the Form 1023, churches applying for recognition of exemption from federal income tax must also provide the IRS with copies of their articles of incorporation and bylaws.

The IRS must respond to the church's application within 120 days following the submission of the application. Usually, however, the church will receive a response within about half that time. Ideally, the church will receive an approval of exemption in the form of a determination letter. However, it is not uncommon for the IRS to forward the organization or its attorney a list of additional questions. Presuming that the organization's answer are submitted in a timely fashion and the answers are satisfactory, the organization should expect to receive its letter of determination within about a month after submitting its answer.

How does a church maintain its tax exempt status?

While maintaining "non-profit" status primarily requires compliance with state law, maintaining federal income tax exemption requires compliance with rules established under the Internal Revenue Code and enforced by the IRS. These rules, taken as a whole, require non-profit organizations to function for "exempt purposes," including charitable, religious, or educational purposes. Specifically, in order to function for exempt purposes, churches should: (a) engage in no substantial political activity; (b) refrain from supporting or opposing any candidate for political office; (c) avoid activities which generate income subject to the tax on unrelated business income (UBIT); and (d) participate in no acts of private inurement.

A.ENGAGE IN NO SUBSTANTIAL POLITICAL ACTIVITY

Churches are permitted to engage in political activities, as long as activities associated with particular pieces of legislation do not represent a "substantial" part of the church's activities or expenses. For example, as long as its efforts to influence legislation are not "substantial," a church may (a) prepare and distribute literature addressing political issues of interest to the organization; (b) advocate a particular stance on social or political issues; (c) attempt to mold public opinion; (d) conduct nonpartisan voter registration drives; and (e) conduct forums designed to educate voters on political issues.

Some charities and religious organizations—but not churches— are permitted to elect a specific numeric ceiling on lobbying expenditures. Unfortunately, outside of this election, there is no rule or formula specifically defining when a political activity associated with a particular piece of legislation is "substantial." However, some legal opinions suggest that no more than about five percent of a religious organization's time, efforts, and financial resources should consist of attempting to influence legislation.

Although the above rules restrict political activities in regard to any particular piece of legislation, the law does not restrict churches from ministering regarding religious issues with political or social implications. For example, if a church intended to lobby in favor of a particular Congressional bill to stop partial birth abortions, the church would need to make sure that its lobbying efforts did not qualify as "substantial." However, there is no restriction limiting the church's ability to preach against abortion in general. Churches are unrestricted in their ability to address issues having political overtones, such as civil rights, abortion, pornography, or divorce, as long as they address these issues without reference to particular pieces of pending legislation.

B. DO NOT SUPPORT OR OPPOSE ANY CANDIDATE FOR POLITICAL OFFICE

Federal law prohibits churches from supporting or opposing any candidate for political office. According to section 501(c)(3) of the Internal Revenue Code, most non-profit organization may not "participate in or intervene in . . . any political campaign on behalf of (or in opposition to) any candidate for political office."

IRS regulations define a "candidate for political office" to include any individual "who offers himself, or is proposed by others, as a contestant for an elective public office." An individual running for the office of senator, congressman, governor, or President would qualify, as would an individual seeking election as a judge, member of the school board, or member of the city council or board of alderman. Former politicians and politicians not currently engaged in a political campaign are not considered "candidates" under this rule.

Under the rules regarding political campaigns, churches may not: (a) permit candidates to distribute campaign literature on church premises; (b) permit candidates to use church facilities to conduct rallies; (c) provide candidates with church mailing lists to contact potential supporters or volunteers; (d) endorse or oppose any political candidate in writing or from the pulpit; (e) make donations to a candidate's campaign; or (f) link a church website to the site of a candidate or a political party. Church leaders must also refrain from endorsing or opposing any candidate on church premises or when acting in their official capacity as representative of their church. Churches are permitted to conduct non-partisan voter education activities, such as distributing non-partisan voter education guides discussing the voting records of the candidates, or even conducting non-partisan debates or question-and-answer forums where the candidates or their representatives attend.

Recently, the IRS has warned churches against participation in political campaigns, and the IRS even revoked the exemption of one church which published an ad opposing the re-election of President Clinton. A single violation of the rule against participation in political campaigns could result in the termination of the organization's federal income tax exemption.

C. AVOID UBIT AND PRIVATE INUREMENT

Finally, in order to maintain federal income tax-exemption and good standing with the Internal Revenue Service, churches should avoid participating in activities which generate income subject to the tax on unrelated business income and refrain from participating in any act of private inurement. Both of these concepts are discussed at length in the following sections.

What is unrelated business income tax (UBIT)?

Churches should avoid engaging in activities which may generate income subject to unrelated business income tax (UBIT). Not only could substantial activities of this nature cause the church to lose its income tax exemption, but the generation of income subject to UBIT will remove the church's statutory shield against IRS audit. The IRS is prohibited from auditing churches under most circumstances. However, this prohibition is removed in the event that the church generates income subject to UBIT.

A. GENERAL DEFINITION

As a general rule, income from activities of tax-exempt organization are subject to UBIT if each of three conditions are met:

1. The income is from a "trade or business." The term, "trade or business," generally includes any activity carried on for the production of income from selling goods or performing services.

2. The trade or business is "regularly carried on" by the organization. Business activities of a tax-exempt organization ordinarily will be considered regularly carried on if they show a frequency and continuity and are carried on in a manner similar to compara-

ble commercial activities of for-profit organizations. Thus, an activity may be regularly carried on if it is conducted on a weekly, monthly, or even annual, basis. Activities are less likely to be considered regularly carried on if they are more random in nature.

3.The trade or business is not "substantially related" to the church's performance of its exempt religious, charitable, or educational purposes. The church's activities must "contribute importantly" to the accomplishment of the organization's exempt purposes. Under IRS rules, a trade or business is related to exempt purposes only when the conduct of the business activities has a causal relationship to the achievement of the exempt purposes. It is important to note that this causal relationship is not established merely by showing that the activities generate income needed by the organization. Thus, if a church operates a convenience store, the church will not be able to avoid the assessment of UBIT simply because all of the profits of the store are used to fund church outreaches. It is the nature of the activity itself, not the use of the funds, which determines whether an activity is subject to UBIT.

B.EXEMPT ACTIVITIES

Several types of activities are exempted from the UBIT rules and thus not subject to the assessment of UBIT.

1.Activities conducted primarily for the convenience of members are not subject to UBIT. For example, the sale of mints, candies, bookmarks, or similar items at church bookstores is generally not subject to UBIT, since such sales are intended primarily to serve and benefit the members at church. This does not mean, however, that any business merely made available to members is excepted from the UBIT rules. Instead, activities must address a bona fide need of the organization's members.

2.An activity in which substantially all of the work is performed for the organization by volunteers is not subject to UBIT. For example, the sale of cookies or magazine subscriptions by a church youth group would likely not be subject to UBIT, since the activity is carried on primarily by volunteers.

3.Sales of donated merchandise are excluded from the UBIT rules. In order for this exception to apply, substantially all of the merchandise sold must have been received by the organization as gifts or contributions. This exception from the UBIT rules is useful to protect church bizarres, raffles, and even thrift shops from the assessment of UBIT.

4.UBIT does not apply to income generated by a church from renting its mailing list to another non-profit and tax-exempt organization.

C.EXEMPT INCOME

In addition to the types of activities listed above, several types of income are exempted from the assessment of UBIT.

1.Interest is exempt, as are dividends from stock that is not "debt-financed." An asset is "debt-financed" if it is subject to a mortgage or "acquisition indebtedness" at any time during the year. Thus, if a church takes out a loan to fund the purchase of Wal-Mart stock, the church must pay UBIT on a dividend paid by Wal-Mart on the stock. However, if the church purchased the stock from its own funds and without borrowing, no UBIT is assessed on the dividend.

2.Royalties are also generally free from the assessment of UBIT, as long as the asset generating the royalty is not debt-financed. In order to be considered a royalty, a payment must be made in exchange for the use of a "valuable intangible property right." For example, a royalty may include payments received by a church from the company which the church has authorized to use the church's name or logo in solicitations of church members.

3.Income from renting church property is another significant type of income that is not subject to UBIT. For example, as a general rule, a church is able to lease out its sanctuary or a parsonage without the assessment of UBIT. However, several cautions apply. First, rental income is subject to UBIT when the leased property is debt-financed. Thus, leasing a mortgaged sanctuary may generate UBIT, presuming that the lease arrangement is "regularly carried on", as discussed above. The lease of the sanctuary would not generate UBIT if the church owned the sanctuary outright and without a mortgage. To further complicate the issue, the IRS will not consider a property to be debt-financed in the rental context if eighty-five percent (85%) or more of the use of property (in terms of square footage or the total hours of use) advances the organization's exempt purposes. This caveat to the debt-financing rule allows churches to regularly lease small portions of their property, such as for weddings, without assessment of UBIT.

4.Rental income from the renting of church property will also not be considered debt-financed in the case of the "neighborhood land rule." The neighborhood land rule provides that if a church acquires real property (i.e., land or buildings) with the intention of using the property for religious, charitable, or educational purposes within fifteen years from the date of its acquisition, the property will not be treated as debt-financed. This rule requires the church to evidence to the IRS after the first five years of ownership of the property that the IRS may be reasonably certain that the property will be used for exempt purposes before the end of the fifteen year period. In order to meet this requirement, the church must prepare a detailed written plan specifying improvements to the property and an intended completion date for those improvements. At least ninety days prior to the end of the fifth year after acquisition of the property, the church should submit this plan to the IRS for a ruling. Unfortunately, the church's plan must include the demolition or destruction, within the fifteen-year period, of the structures on the property which are not used for religious or charitable purposes. (Note that in the case of ministries, the property must be used within ten years and must be located within one mile of the ministry's other facilities.)

Another general caution that applies in the context of rental arrangements pertains to rents received from a corporation controlled by a church. Churches which own for-profit subsidiaries, discussed below, should generally avoid receiving rent from the subsidiary, since rent received from a for-profit corporation which is owned or controlled by a church is considered income subject to UBIT for the church.

Churches should also be aware that leases of personal property along with real estate are generally subject to UBIT. Rents from personal property (i.e., movable items such as tables, chairs, and certain sound equipment) leased with real estate are exempted from UBIT, but only if the rents from the personal property represent an "incidental amount" of the total rents received under the lease. As a general rule, rents from personal property will not be considered "incidental" if they exceed 10% of the total rents from the leased property.

As a final caution in the rental context, there is no exemption from UBIT for rental payments attributable to personal services. According to the IRS regulations, "services are considered rendered to the occupant if they are primarily for his convenience and are other than those usually or customarily rendered in connection with the rental of rooms or other space for occupancy only." Thus, maid service would be considered a personal service, whereas heat and light, cleaning of public entrances and exits, trash collection, and general security services probably are not. In order for a church to avoid UBIT on the lease of its property, it should not provide personal services under the lease.

5.Gains and losses from the sale of property, other than items held for sale in the regular course of business (i.e., inventory), are generally excluded from the assessment of UBIT. However, gain from the sale of debt-financed property which was not actually used for exempt religious, educational, or charitable purposes prior to the sale is subject to UBIT if the property was debt-financed at the time of the sale. For this reason, it may be a good idea for a church to pay off its debt on such property and hold the property for at least a year before selling it. Because the property is not considered debt-financed if it is free from a mortgage or acquisition indebtedness for more than a year, gains from a sale after the year would not be subject to UBIT.

D.ADVERTISING REVENUES

Income from advertising, such as the sale of ads in a church magazine or the sale of billboard space, is almost always subject to UBIT. However, "qualified sponsorship payments" are not considered advertising under IRS rules. Under the applicable rules, a company may sponsor a church event by providing the church a charitable gift in exchange for permission to display the company's name, logo, product lines, and slogan at a church event or in a church periodical associated with a particular event. For example, a local restaurant could make a qualified sponsorship payment to a church in exchange for permission to display a banner at a church campmeeting or for the right to be listed as a sponsor on posters advertising the event of programs sold at the event. However, churches are not permitted to display qualitative or comparative language, price information, indications of savings or value, or endorsements or inducements to sell or use a sponsor's products or services.

E.USE OF SUBSIDIARY CORPORATIONS TO SHIELD ACTIVITIES FROM UBIT

If a church intends to enter into an activity that will generate UBIT, the church should consider forming a for-profit subsidiary to engage in the activity. A subsidiary is typically a for-profit corporation, the shares of which are owned by the church. A subsidiary may engage in an activity which would ordinarily generate UBIT for a church, pay taxes on the income from the activity, and pay the remaining income to the church in the form of a dividend. (Payments of rents, royalties, or interest from a subsidiary to its church parent are subject to UBIT; dividends are not.) This method shields the church from UBIT.

Churches should exercise caution to ensure that the subsidiary functions independently from the church and not simply as another church outreach. A subsidiary corporation will be ignored for tax purposes (thus generating UBIT for the church on the subsidiary's income) if the subsidiary has no identity and function independent from the parent corporation. The subsidiary corporation must have some real substantial business function and activity. For example, if a church leases its sanctuary and the lease payments would generate UBIT if received by the church, UBIT is not avoided simply by requiring the tenant to issue the payments to a subsidiary corporation. If the subsidiary has not substantive function in the transaction, such as ownership or management of the facility, the subsidiary will be discarded for tax purposes, and UBIT will be assessed on the church. Thus, a subsidiary should have its own bank accounts; conduct shareholders and directors meetings on its own time and not during church hours; keep its own minutes; hire its own employees (although some such employees may also work for the church on the church's time); process its own payroll; and pay wages and expenses from its own revenues. Also, the subsidiary should not use the church's assets without compensating the church.

F.990-T FILING REQUIREMENT

If a church is unable to avoid generating income subject to UBIT, the church must file an IRS Form 990-T upon generating $1000.00 or more in gross income subject to UBIT. This form must usually be filed by May 15. In some cases, churches are also required to make quarterly estimated payments of UBIT.

What is "private inurement"?

Federal statutes prohibit organizations recognized as exempt from federal income tax from engaging in any act of "private inurement" or any substantial act of "private benefit".

A.GENERAL DEFINITION

Private inurement is defined as transferring of a tax-exempt organization's assets or income to an "insider," except as reasonable payment for goods or services provided to the organization.

Stated a different way, private inurement is the transfer of the assets or income of an exempt organization for private purposes. By contrast, although "private benefit" also involves use of the assets or income of a tax-exempt organization for private purposes, private benefit does not involve an insider. An insider is an individual having a significant voice in the organization's policymaking or significant control over the organization's operations. Trustees, officers, key employees, and even major donors may be considered insiders.

The theoretical consequence of private inurement or substantial acts of private benefit is revocation of federal income tax exemption. The IRS may also levy stiff excise tax penalties against the beneficiary of the transaction, as well as the board members approving the transaction.

B. COMMON CATEGORIES OF INUREMENT AND PRIVATE BENEFIT

There are four basic categories of private inurement or private benefit transactions, including (a) unreasonable borrowing arrangements; (b) unreasonable rental arrangements; (c) issuance of goods or services to private individuals; and (d) unreasonable compensation arrangements. An unreasonable borrowing arrangement is an arrangement under which a church lends money to or borrows money from an insider (in the case of inurement) or another individual or entity (in the case of a private benefit transaction) under terms that are less favorable to the church than the marketplace would dictate for an arm's length transaction. For example, if a church lent money to its pastor without assessing any interest, or if the church loaned him a very large amount without requiring any security for the loan, the IRS would likely consider the transaction an act of private inurement. Or, if a church borrowed money from a member of the community at rate of interest significantly higher than rates which commercial lenders would have offered the church, this transaction may also represent private inurement.

Similarly, under an unreasonable rental arrangement, the church is subjected to lease terms which are disadvantageous to the church and which are not commercially reasonable. For example, if a church rents its meeting facility from its pastor and pays significantly more rent per square foot than average for the area, private inurement is present. Or, if a church permits an employee to use the church facilities for a family reunion without charge and without reporting the value of the usage as taxable income, private benefit may be present.

Churches may sometimes unwittingly engage in acts of private inurement or private benefit when providing goods or services to insiders or to individuals who are not in need of charitable assistance. Churches are, of course, permitted to provide charitable assistance to needy individuals. Churches may make grants of food, clothing, or money, and may also provide valuable services, such as job training or refurbishing and repairing of a home. However, churches must make sure that the recipients of such benevolence are, in fact, poor or needy. For example, in the inurement context, churches sometimes provide services to pastors, such as promoting the pastor's latest book. Presuming that the pastor owns the rights to the book and personally profits from its sale, the church should refrain from such promotion. Similarly, the church should not funnel business to a for-profit business owned by the pastor and should not enter into contracts with the pastor's business, unless, of course, the terms of the contracts are commercially reasonable or favor the church.

It is well-known that non-profit organizations may pay their employees only a reasonable compensation. Payment of excessive compensation to insiders may be considered private inurement and subject the organization to excise tax penalties or even to loss of federal income tax exemption. The topic of compensation of church employees is discussed at length in the following section.

C. REIMBURSEMENT OF EMPLOYEE BUSINESS EXPENSES

Finally, church leaders should keep in mind the rules regarding substantiation of employee business expenses. An employee who incurs a business expense on behalf of his or her church employer is entitled to receive a reimbursement of the expense from the church or to deduct the expense from his or her federal income taxes. However, in order for the employee to receive a reimbursement without the assessment of income taxes on the reimbursement, the reimbursement must be made subject to an "accountable reimbursement plan."

An accountable reimbursement plan is a plan adopted by an employer, usually as a corporate resolution or as part of the corporate bylaws, which requires employees to substantiate their business expenses to their employer within 60 days following the date the expense was incurred. The plan must call for substantiation by written receipt or other documentation establishing the date and nature of the expense. Reimbursements that are not made subject to the terms of an accountable reimbursement plan are considered taxable income, and a church's failure to treat such payments as taxable income technically qualifies as private inurement or private benefit.

What rules apply to establishing compensation for pastors and church employees?

EXCESS BENEFIT TRANSACTIONS

Federal law and recent federal regulations levy stiff excise tax penalties against tax-exempt organizations and their employees participating in or approving "excess benefit transactions." The law provides that employees receiving excessive compensation from a tax-exempt organization may be assessed a tax of 25% of the excess benefit and an additional 200% if the excess benefit is not promptly reimbursed to the organization. Board members knowingly approving of the excess may be assessed a tax of 10% of the excess benefit. These penalties were established in order to provide an alternate penalty for the IRS to utilize instead of revocation of income tax exemption for the organization. Nevertheless, the IRS may still revoke an organization's exemption if an unreasonable compensation arrangement evidences that the organization no longer operates for charitable, educational, or religious purposes.

According to the statute, an "excess benefit transaction" is any transaction in which economic benefit is provided by a tax-exempt organization to a disqualified person if the value of the economic benefit provided to the individual exceeds the value received by the organization in exchange for providing the benefit. A "disqualified person" is a person who was, during the five year period ending on the date of the excess benefit transaction, in a position to exercise substantial influence over the affairs of the organization.

B.COMPENSATION MUST BE REASONABLE

Clearly, pastors meet the definition of disqualified persons. Thus, a tax-exempt organization may not sell items or services to a minister at a price that is less than fair market value; purchase items or services from the minister for more than fair market value; or permit the minister to use the organization's property without receiving adequate compensation—in the form of money or services—in return. Nor may a church or ministry pay its minister compensation that exceeds the minister's value to the organization. As stated by the IRS in its proposed regulations, "Compensation paid may not exceed what is reasonable under the circumstances. Compensation for the performance of services is reasonable if it is only such amount as would ordinarily be paid for like services by like enterprises under like circumstances."

IRS proposed regulations state that certain "revenue-sharing transactions" may qualify as prohibited excess benefit transactions. According to the rules, a "revenue-sharing transaction" is a transaction in which the economic benefit provided to the disqualified person is determined in whole or in part by the revenues of one or more of the organization's activities. One example would be an arrangement under which a pastor is permitted to manage his church's investments in exchange for a percentage of the profits generated from those investments. Another example would be a royalty payment arrangement in which a minister is given a royalty by his ministry on the sale of books he writes for the ministry. And yet another example would be an arrangement whereby a pastor is paid a percentage of the donations made to his church.

It may come as a surprise that under the proposed regulations, not all revenue-sharing transactions are prohibited. According to the regulations, the key consideration is whether the payment arrangement permits the minister to receive additional compensation without providing proportional benefits to the organization in order to further the charitable or religious purposes of the organization. If the revenue-sharing transaction permits the minister to receive more income without providing a proportional benefit to the organization, the transaction will be considered illegal. For example, under the first example provided above, if the percentage of the minister's share of the profits increases automatically each year whether or not the value of the investments has increased, the transaction will likely be considered an illegal excess benefit transaction. Likewise, the transaction will likely be prohibited if the minister does not manage the investments, yet still receives a percentage of their increase in value.

Ministers should keep in mind the following rules of thumb regarding impermissible excess benefit transactions: (a) Financial transactions between a minister and his church or ministry should be approved by the governing body of the organization or a committee of the governing body composed entirely of individuals who are not parties to the transaction and have no conflict of interest associated with it; (b) Ministers should pay market value or more for any property or service received from the church, unless the property or service is provided as reasonable compensation for services provided to the organization by the minister; and (c) Ministers should avoid arrangements which make the amount of payment to the minister contingent upon the amount of income received by the organization from a ministry activity. If such a payment arrangement is undertaken, the minister's compensation should not increase unless the minister first provides a proportional increase in benefits to the organization.

C. COMPENSATION COMMITTEES CREATE PRESUMPTION OF REASONABLENESS

The excise tax penalties for excessive compensation create a strong incentive for pastors to ensure that the amount of their compensation is reasonable. Fortunately, the law provides a system through which a pastor can establish a "rebuttable presumption" that his compensation is reasonable. The establishment of a rebuttable presumption requires the IRS to prove that the compensation is not reasonable—-rather than requiring the pastor to prove that his compensation is reasonable.

Under the law, setting a minister's compensation, including salary, housing allowance, and other benefits, through an independent compensation committee that relies on "comparability data" creates a rebuttable presumption that the level of compensation is reasonable. In order to be considered "independent," the compensation committee must be composed of individuals that are not compensated by the corporation or subject to the direct authority of the individual whose compensation is being set. This means that employees of the church should not be on the committee. Ideally, the committee members should also be chosen based upon their experience and expertise in ministry, business, or in setting executive compensation.

To ascertain reasonable compensation, the committee should consider the average compensation enjoyed by other ministers with similar education, years of experience, hours worked, and scope of duties, in organizations of similar size located in a socioeconomically comparable areas. In addition to their own personal knowledge of compensation levels, the committee members should consult national compensation surveys. It is also a good idea for the committee to rely upon compensation recommendations from an attorney or accountant experienced in pastoral compensation. Small organizations (those whose annual receipts are less than $1,000,000) may satisfy the rule requiring review of comparability data simply by obtaining data on compensation paid by three comparable organizations for similar services in similar communities.

After consulting its comparability data and approving the compensation, the committee should carefully document its decision in minutes. The minutes should identify the effective date of the approval, the duration for which the compensation was approved, the names of the committee members, and, most importantly, the factors and considerations, including the pertinent comparability data, which served as the basis for the setting of the compensation.

D. GENERAL RULES REGARDING DESIGNATION OF HOUSING ALLOWANCE

The Internal Revenue Code permits licensed or ordained ministers to receive a housing allowance as part of their compensation for ministerial services. A housing allowance is a portion of income that is not subject to federal income taxes. It is important to remember, however, that the housing allowance, although exempt from federal income taxes, is still subject to self-employment taxes—unless the minister has obtained exemption from social security taxes.

The amount of a minister's housing allowance is established by the board, committee, or individual charged with the duty of setting the minister's compensation. Housing allowance designations must be applied prospectively. Thus, a church may not make a retroactive decision to treat a portion of the compensation previously paid to a minister as housing allowance.

For years, the Internal Revenue Service has stated that the amount of a minister's housing allowance exempt from the assessment of federal income taxes is equal to the lesser of: (a) the amount actually used to provide a home; (b) the amount officially designated by the employer as a housing allowance; and (c) the fair rental value of the home, including costs of furnishings and utilities. However, in Warren v. Commissioner, 114 T.C. No. 23 (2000), the United States Tax Court held that the fair rental value limitation is invalid. The importance of this decision is that, if upheld by the various Courts of Appeals, the decision would permit a minister to take as much housing allowance in the year as the amount of his or her housing expenses in the year, even if this amount exceeds the fair rental value of the home. For example, a minister would be permitted to spend significant funds on a down payment to purchase a home, on refurbishing a home, or on paying off a home mortgage, and treat the same amount of his or her income in the year as housing allowance.

The IRS has appealed this decision to the Ninth Circuit Court of Appeals. The Ninth Circuit has not yet issued its decision, but could affirm or reverse the decision of the Tax Court. If the Ninth Circuit overturns the Tax Court's decision, ministers who have ignored the fair rental value limitation may be required to pay income taxes on their excess housing allowance. The IRS may also appeal the decision to the ten other federal appeals courts. The Ninth Circuit, which has not been sympathetic to other highly-visible IRS appeals in the past, has jurisdiction over the states of Alaska, Arizona, California, Hawaii, Idaho, Montana, Nevada, Oregon, and Washington and the territories of the Northern Mariana Islands and Guam.

What rules apply to fundraising and the deductibility of donations?

As a general rule, a donor's gift of cash property is deductible on the donor's federal income tax return if the donor is able to itemize his or her deductions. The amount of the deduction which the donor is entitled to enjoy depends in part on the type of donation that the donor makes.

A. GIFTS OF CASH

For an individual's gifts of cash to a church, the maximum amount which he or she may deduct in a year is an amount equal to 50% of his or her adjusted gross income for the year. The remaining amount of the donation, if any, may be carried over and deducted sometime during the following five years. For example, a donor with adjusted gross income of $100,000 may deduct up to $50,000 in gifts to his church for a single year. Of course, if the donor gave less than $50,000, the amount of his deduction is less. Thus, if the donor has $100,000 in adjusted gross income in 2001 and gives $20,000 in cash gifts to his church and makes no other charitable gifts, the amount of his allowable deduction is $20,000. If instead, he gave $60,000 to his church, he may receive a $50,000 deduction on his taxes for the year the donation was made and carry over the remaining $10,000 to deduct sometime in the following five years.

Gifts of cash by corporations are deductible up to 10% of the corporation's adjusted gross income for the year.

B. GIFTS OF PROPERTY

The rules pertaining to gifts of property are a bit more complicated. As a general rule, the amount of an individual's deduction for gifts of property to a church is limited to 30% of his or her adjusted gross income. (Note that the 30% limitation discussed here in not cumulative with the 50% limitation discussed above in the case of an individual who gives both cash and property. Special formulas are used to blend the limitations and to calculate the exact limit in such a case.) Thus, if the taxpayer discussed above gave a home valued at $50,000 to his church and made no other charitable gifts, he could receive a deduction of $30,000 this year and carry over the remaining $20,000 to be used during the following five years.

Like gifts of cash, gifts of property by corporations are deductible up to 10% of the corporation's adjusted gross income for the year.

There are two possible means of valuing a gift of property for purposes of determining the amount of a deduction. In some cases, the value of the gift is the owner's "basis" in the property, while in other cases, the value of the gift is the fair market value of the property. A property is generally valued at its basis (the amount that the donor paid for the property) if (a) the donor has owned the property for less than one year prior to donating it, or (b) the donation is tangible personal property (property other than land or buildings or stock) and is used by the church for some purpose other than the church's charitable, educational, or religious purposes.

Property is usually valued at its fair market value if the donor owns the property for a year or more prior to making the donation. Thus, a gift of a home owned for less than a year is valued for deduction purposes at the amount the donor paid for the home, while the home is valued at its fair market value for deduction purposes if the donor owns the home for more than a year before making the gift.

C. GIFTS OF SERVICES OR A PARTIAL INTEREST IN PROPERTY

Gifts of services are not deductible for the donor. For example, an attorney, accountant, or painter who donates her services to a church is not entitled to receive any tax deduction for her time. Also, gifts of a "partial interest" in property (i.e., where the donor retains ownership interest in the property) are not deductible. This means that a property owner is not entitled to a deduction for permitting a church to lease facilities for little or no rent. Nor is a business entitled to receive a charitable deduction for lending equipment, such as a forklift, truck, or sound equipment to a church.

D. QUID PRO QUO GIFTS

"Quid pro quo" gifts are only partially deductible for the donor. A quip pro quo gift is a gift which is given in partial exchange for something of value. For example, if a donor gives a gift of $50 and receives in exchange a book or tape series, the gift is considered a quid pro quo gift. In such case, the value of the donation for deduction purposes is generally the difference between the total amount of the donation and the value of the gift received in exchange. However, certain quid pro quo gifts are considered fully deductible. The current rule, which is indexed annually for inflation, provides that the full amount of the donor's gift is deductible if: (a) the fair market value of all of the benefits received in connection with the payment, is not more than two percent of the payment, or $76, whichever is less, or (b) the payment is $38 or more and the only benefits received in connection with the payment are token items (bookmarks, calendars, key chains, mugs, posters, tee shirts, etc.) bearing the organization's name or logo and valued in the aggregate at no more than $7.60.

E. DESIGNATED DONATIONS

Churches are often asked to accept donations which are earmarked for specific projects or specific people. Gifts designated for a particular project, such as a building fund, are generally deductible by the donor. Churches are also required to honor the designation made by the donor. However, many churches prefer not to accept designated donations, preferring instead to retain the authority to direct income to whatever areas the church leadership deems necessary.

If a church desires to remove a designation on a gift already made, the church may obtain a release from the original donor and in some cases may even obtain release by a court. In order to avoid designations on new donations, a church should inform donors that the church will not honor designations and that the church reserves the right to redirect donations to the area of greatest need. This policy should be written on church offering envelopes, bulletins, and/or magazines so that potential donors are made aware of the policy. In the case that the church still receives designated donations, the church should communicate its policy directly to donors before the donation is deposited, so that the donor is afforded the opportunity to release the designation or revoke the donation.

As a general rule, churches should not accept donations designated for particular individuals, since such donations are not deductible by the donor. Even in the case of gifts designated for poor or needy individuals, the law prohibits a deduction for the donor. In order for the donor to obtain an income tax deduction, the gift must be made to or for the use of the tax-exempt organization to which the gift is given. Thus, if a donor desires to give a charitable gift to a particular needy individual, the person should give the gift directly to that person and not claim a deduction for the gift. Or, the person may give the gift to his church and designate the gift for benevolence purposes. The church may then make its own determination of the best recipient of the gift. This method allows the donor to receive a deduction, even if the church sometimes chooses the same charitable recipient which the donor originally intended.

Gifts designated for missionaries or individuals traveling on short term missions trips are generally excepted from the rules prohibiting deductions for gifts designated for particular individuals. Donors are entitled to a tax deduction for donations designated for the use of missionaries if the recipient organization exercises oversight over the use of the funds by the missionary. The church should require the missionary to report to the church at least quarterly on the use of the funds sent to the missionary. Any funds used by the missionary for personal expenses, rather than for ministry (i.e., crusades, Bibles, gifts of food or clothing to the poor) should be treated as income for which the missionary should be issued a Form 1099. Gifts funding short term missions trips are deductible, as long as the church uses the funds for ministry purposes and not to fund personal expenses, such as entertainment, clothing, or souvenirs for the individuals taking the trip.

F. SUBSTANTIATION OF CONTRIBUTIONS

Church leaders should keep in mind several rules regarding substantiation of the donor's gifts. The most important rule to remember is that churches must issue their donors receipts for donations of cash or property valued at $250 or more by the due date (plus extensions) of the donor's income tax return. The receipt must be written and must include: (a) the amount of cash contributed, (b) a description of any property contributed, (c) a statement of whether the church gave the donor any goods or services in return for the donations, and (d) a description and good faith estimate of the value of any such goods or services given to the donor in return for the donations. If the only benefit that the donor received was an intangible religious benefit, the receipt should say so, without attempting to describe or estimate the value of the benefit.

If a church receives a quid pro quo contribution in excess of $75, the church must issue a receipt, and the receipt must: (a) inform the donor that the amount of the contribution that is deductible is the excess of the amount of the donation over the value of the goods or services provided by the organization, and (b) provide the donor with a good faith estimate of the value of the goods or services.

Donors giving property to their church often request that the church list the value of the property on the gift receipt. However, the law provides that the donor—not the church—is required to value the property for deduction purposes. When providing a receipt for a donation of property, a church should describe the property and comply with the other receipt requirements addressed above. The donor then determines the value of the property on his own. For property valued at $500 or more, the donor must complete an IRS Form 8283 and provide the form to the IRS when he files his tax returns. IRS rules also require the donor to obtain a qualified written appraisal for property valued by the donor at $5000 or more. This appraisal will be summarized and documented on a portion of the Form 8283.

CHAPTER THREE

MAXIMIZING YOUR REAL ESTATE

Curtis W. Wallace

What is the biggest investment that your church is likely to make? In most cases, the answer is the same — your real estate. Every church, whether growing or shrinking, experiences constant change and that change translates to the facilities that the church occupies. This results in the one common denominator that all church pastors and administrators face, the challenge of managing real estate.

At some point in time, every church faces the need to either buy land to build a new building, sell an existing property, renovate a building or finance its property. With this need in mind, this chapter explores the key principles involved with acquiring, developing, selling and managing your organization's real estate.

Understanding the concepts explored here will greatly aid your efforts. Because of the significant dollars involved in any real estate deal of any size, everyone involved in the process from brokers, to contractors, to city officials, to bankers, share a common credential — they are typically all full-time industry professionals. The people you will deal with spend their days working in real estate. Consequently, they often have a great deal of knowledge; knowledge that non-professionals typically lack.

It is how you and the group of professionals that you hire use that knowledge that will determine, in large part, the success of your project. Too often, mistakes are made in assembling or managing the team that will bring your project to fruition. The common results are disputes, drama and lost money. Many times, the losses and headaches are caused by the church's attempt to save a few bucks on the front-end and not employing qualified professionals to guide them. Other times, churches let the wrong professional drive the entire process.

One point that cannot be over-emphasized is simple - trust should come slow and be earned. Real estate is real business with real risk and success requires the right team. That team should be engaged based on their qualifications and merits, not their affiliations.

One of the most common mistakes that churches make when engaging in real estate transactions is to select team members based on their standing in the church or their appeal to your heart. For good reason, all of us want to do business with Christians. Certainly you can trust someone whose Christian "connections and credentials" are clearly established. But be wary. Too many unsavory business people wrap their true intent in the clothing of Christianity.

Here is a word to the wise on this topic. When the people who are trying to earn your business spend more time talking about church and the Lord than they do talking about the subject of the meeting — your building — then you may have a problem. While it is natural to discuss common interests and develop a relationship with someone, serious business people will always get down to business. A legitimate builder, for example, will want to talk about what he has done, the buildings he has built and why he is right man for the job. Be careful when someone is slow getting down to business — there may be a reason he or she wants to gloss over the business side of things.

Given that real estate is a complicated, often sophisticated, industry, it is not possible for the church staff to do everything. The best role for the church staff to take is the management of the overall process. To do so, it is critical to understand the process, how each player fits into that process, how the players interact and, most importantly, how each player is compensated and the likely goals of that player.

Accordingly, throughout this chapter, I will highlight the steps in the process and explain who the players are and who is responsible for what. This will, hopefully, provide insight into the process and highlight the potential problem areas. At the end of the day, you will be in a position to guide your organization and manage your advisors, rather than have them manage you.

Because the issues and problems faced in each scenario are different, this chapter will separately discuss the challenges of new church construction, purchasing an existing building, selling property, and financing your purchase and/or construction.

Purchase of an Existing Facility

Of the options to be covered, the purchase of an existing facility is by far the simplest process. By contrast, the number of unknowns and, consequently, the complexity multiplies for the construction of a new facility. Nonetheless, ample opportunity exists for the unwary to be taken advantage of and to not get what they bargained for. The following is an outline of the basic steps to be followed.

Determining How Much You Can Afford

Before you go shopping, you need to know what you can afford. If you skip this step, you are very likely to waste a lot of time. Moreover, you are likely to waste the time of a lot of other people who have spent time, money and effort chasing a deal that you could never close in the first place. Such failed endeavors will harm your reputation in the real estate community and make everything you try later more difficult. You can quickly be labeled as a "flake" and the best people will avoid working with you.

A few simple rules of thumb will help you establish a ballpark budget. If your organization only wants to pay cash for its building, this analysis is fast and simple — how much cash do you have now and how much more can you raise before you make the purchase. However, the cash real estate buyer is clearly the exception to the rule and even the largest churches typically obtain long-term financing for most of the purchase price of real estate acquisitions.

Therefore, the big question is really how much money can you or should you borrow to help finance your purchase. First, you should know that traditional lenders (e.g. commercial banks) evaluate loans to religious organizations based on two primary factors; the value of the underlying collateral (what is the building you are buying worth) and on the strength of your church's cash flow stream (how much excess cash do you have available each month to pay your mortgage).

Collateral Value

The value of your collateral is critical because banks will typically only loan a certain percentage of a property's value. By loaning less than the full value of the property, the bank lowers its risk and protects itself in the event that the borrower defaults. The reasoning is that if the banks forecloses on the property and resells it, the property will be worth more than the amount owed on the loan. While each lender evaluates loans differently and churches vary as to how conservative they want to be from a debt perspective, most lenders will want a loan to value ratio of approximately sixty to eighty percent (60%-80%), with the most common loan to value ratio being 75%. The loan to value ratio is the amount of the loan as a percentage of the property's appraised value. The number is calculated by dividing the loan amount by the appraised value. Therefore, a loan of $7,500,000 on a property that has an appraised value of $10,000,000 has a loan to value ratio of 75%.

The importance of the bank's loan to value ratio is that it determines the minimum amount of the down payment that is required to make the purchase. If your lender requires a 75% loan to value ratio, at least 25% of the purchase price will have to be paid in cash (or additional collateral will have to be pledged). In terms of your organization's situation, the loan to value ratio will give a quick indication of how expensive of a building you can afford to purchase. For example, if your organization has $2,000,000 of excess cash to use for a down-payment, the organization could, at most, afford an $8,000,000 property if the lender employs a 75% loan to value ratio.

At this point, a word to the wise is in order. When trying to assess what you can afford, it is very important to be conservative and leave yourself a cushion. You may be glad you have added flexibility for two reasons. First, there are always surprises when you move into a new facility. From unexpected repair bills to new furniture, phone systems and sound equipment purchases, the purchase of the building is just the start of the expenses and you should plan accordingly. Second, loan to value ratios are typically based on appraised values, not the purchase price of the property. Frequently, churches run into trouble when an appraisal comes in at a lower than expected value and creates an unplanned shortfall in the loan amount. Therefore, leave yourself some wiggle room in case you do not get the value you expect.

Most appraisers view churches as special purpose facilities with a limited resale market. The result is that appraisers cannot assess the value of a church as accurately as they judge the value of an office building. The result is that many appraisers significantly discount the value of churches resulting in low appraisals.

The conservative approach of many appraisers is a result of the three primary methods that appraisers use to assess value and the difficulty in applying those methods to churches. Appraisers use three methods to calculate property values — the income approach, the comparable sales approach, and the replacement cost approach.

The income approach values a property based on the income stream that the property can generate over time. For example, if an office building can generate $1,000,000 a year in rents and the building cost $300,000 to operate, the building generates yearly income of $700,000. In turn the building can be valued based on rates of return desired by investors. An investor desiring a 10% annual return would, in theory, pay $7,000,000 to get a building with an income stream of $700,000.

Unfortunately, the income method is not readily applicable to churches. There is not an active market for church rentals and, as a result, most churches do not generate any significant income. Therefore, the income approach is useless.

However, this is changing for some large mega churches. Large churches that can be used as event centers do have the potential to generate significant income even if they do not house a church. In such cases, it may be helpful to provide the appraiser with rental information and rates on comparable facilities in your area.

In fact, it is this ability to be used as an event center that motivates some lenders to make mega-church loans in the first place. For instance, Bank of America financed both the Potter's House as well as Bishop Ulmer's purchase of the LA Forum. In both cases, the rental capacity of the buildings was a significant factor in lowering the bank's ultimate risk and, consequently, making the loan attractive to the bank.

The second method used by appraisers is the comparable sales approach. Under this approach, the appraiser attempts to identify properties that have recently sold that are similar to the property that you are buying. The appraiser will attempt to learn what the comparable properties sold for and will then make up and down adjustments to that price to account for differences between the properties (one is bigger, one is newer, one included sound equipment, etc.) to arrive at a market value for the property you are buying. The problem with this approach is the relatively small numbers of churches for sale in a given area usually don't sell within a close time period (sales two years ago have little relevance to today's values). Accordingly, you may have to use your superior knowledge of the church world to help an appraiser obtain good data.

The third approach is the replacement cost approach. Under this method, the appraiser uses readily available construction cost data to estimate the likely cost to rebuild or replace the building you are buying. When added to the raw land value, this gives you the replacement cost of the property. The appraiser then will usually employ a discount to account for the age of the building to arrive at a market value.

As you can see, each of the three approaches has shortcomings. For that reason and because church are special purpose buildings (for the most part only churches want a church building), most appraisers tend to apply significant discounts to the value they reach using the three above approaches. As previously stated, it is this "off the top" discount that often results in lower than expected appraisals.

In addition to the loan to value ratio, the lender will look at your church's Debt Service Ratio. While lenders use varying definitions, the debt service ratio is generally defined as your organization's annual cash flow (income less operating expenses) divided by your organization's annual debt service obligations (including all lease payments and the debt service payments on the new loan you are seeking). Therefore, if your annual cash flow is $2,000,000 and your debt service requirements are $1,250,000, your debt service ratio is 1.6 ($2,000,000 divided by $1,250,000).

Most lenders will require a Debt Service Ratio of at least 1.5. This is to insure that the organization has plenty of cash to pay its ordinary expenses and service its debt obligations. In other words, the bank is looking at the strength of your church's cash flow. For many banks that understand church lending, this is the most important decision making tool. The bank is determining how strong the cash flow is and how likely is that cash flow stream to continue.

It is because the bank is trying to assess the likely strength of your church's future cash flow that they want to look at your historical cash flow and make judgments about the ability of your leadership. Your past performance tells the bank if your church is growing, shrinking or maintaining status quo. The bank looks at your leadership team to judge the likelihood that your church will experience traumatic difficulty that will negatively impact cash flow.

A strong management team will make up for a lot of other shortcomings when a banker analyzes a deal. The bank knows that a strong management team will not only avoid problems, but also deal effectively with problems when they do surface. For this reason, the "get to know you" meetings that bankers love to have are very important. The meeting is an interview, and you should act accordingly.

At this point, let's work through an example for determining how much a sample church can afford. Here are the assumptions for our calculations:

Required Loan to Value Ratio-75%

Minimum Debt Service Ratio-1.5

Available Cash for Down Payment-$1,000,000

Annual Cash Flow (income minus expenses)-$600,000

Annual Debt Service Obligations (excluding building loan)-$100,000

Based on the loan to value ratio, the most expensive building this church can afford is $4,000,000 (with a loan to value ratio of 75%, a down-payment of 25% is required and the $1,000,000 cash on hand is 25% of $4,000,000). Based on the Debt Service Ratio, the church can afford annual debt payments for the building of $300,000 or monthly payments of $25,000 (the cash flow of $600,000 divided by the debt service ratio of 1.5, minus the other debt service obligations of $100,000 per year). Given current rates, your accountant or banker can quickly tell you how large of a loan can be supported with monthly payments of $25,000. However, for a quick ballpark guess, multiply the monthly payment by 100. In this case, the cash flow of the church will support a loan in the $2,500,000 range and, when the down payment is added, the church's budget should be in the $3,500,000 range.

Finding the Property/Using a Broker

Now that you know what you can afford, you need to find properties that meet your needs and budget. If you are planning to buy an existing property, one option is to retain a qualified real estate broker to help you identify possibilities. A good broker will not only be able to help identify possible properties that meet your needs, but also help you evaluate the properties market value and negotiate a good deal. However, a note of warning is warranted here. Like all other professionals, real estate brokers come in two varieties, good and bad. A knowledgeable broker who has experience in handling church transactions will be invaluable and from the viewpoint of the buyer, is typically cost free because most sellers will pay the broker's commission. Moreover, a good broker will be able to help you through the entire process. The broker should have contacts in the lending community and with others that you will need in order to help with the process. However, a bad broker who is only interested in closing a deal and making a fee will often lead you into bad deals.

The critical first step in working with your broker is clearly defining who the broker represents. Even though the seller will typically pay the broker, you need to have an agreement that clearly states that the broker represents you as the buyer and only you. I strongly advise against entering into any arrangement where the broker represents both sides of the deal. You need someone you can trust to protect your interests and only your interests. When the broker also represents the seller, you never who the broker is looking out for and you should not put yourself in the position of taking chances.

If you are only interested in purchasing an existing church facility, you may be able to proceed without a broker. You may be able to find a suitable property through your church's sphere of influence in the larger church community of your area. Quite often, churches come onto the sale market because of the natural evolutionary process that churches go through. On-going population shifts cause churches and congregations to change over time. As a community changes, certain churches in that area experience congregational declines while others experience tremendous congregational growth. As a result, a market develops as some churches need smaller quarters, others need larger buildings, and some want to build or relocate. Therefore, knowledge of what other churches are doing can present opportunities to make attractive deals.

Once you have entered into a representation agreement with a qualified broker or identified someone else to aid your search, make sure he or she understands your goals and objectives and let them do their job. The broker should identify and bring to you a list of possibilities that meet your needs. Then you can begin to narrow the choices and when you find the right one, begin to negotiate the right deal.

Putting the Deal Together

After you have found that perfect property, you need to negotiate and document your deal. With regard to negotiation, your broker should be providing you with the values of comparable properties to help you decide what to offer. However, always consider the broker's motivation. He gets paid when a deal closes. As a result, some brokers may push you to offer a little more than you should so that the seller will jump at the deal and the broker will get paid.

Next, remember that there is more to negotiate than price. Your ability to close quickly can provide significant motivation to a seller. Similarly, you may be willing to pay the seller's price if the seller is providing attractive seller financing. The main point to remember is that EVERYTHING is negotiable. There are no rules for real estate deals. Just because something has not been done before is not a reason not to try.

At the same time that you are negotiating the deal, you are beginning to document the deal. Typically, a commercial real estate deal is documented in two steps. First, the buyer or the buyer's lawyer prepares and sends a letter of intent to the seller. A letter of intent is a simple one to two page non-binding letter that merely evidences the intent of the parties to enter into a formal contract. The purpose of a letter of intent is to establish the commitment of the parties to enter into a deal on certain terms, before the parties go to the greater expense of drafting and negotiating a formal purchase contract.

The letter of intent will typically set forth the following items:

The purchase price to be paid for the property

The amount of the earnest money deposit (typically 1-5% of the proposed purchase price) to be put up by the buyer when the contract is signed

The manner in which the price is to be paid (will the buyer pay cash at closing or is seller financing involved)

The contingencies involved in the deal (is the deal dependent upon the buyer obtaining financing from a third party or upon the buyer selling its existing facility first)

The timing of the deal including the length of buyer's feasibility period (how long the buyer has to study the property and perform tests to determine if the property is suitable) and when the closing will occur

A period for buyer's review of seller's title to determine if the seller can convey good title to the property, who is going to pay for title insurance, and the survey of the property

In addition to the above points (which are typically non-binding in a letter of intent) a good attorney will option add two provisions which are meant to bind the parties:

A statement that the terms of the letter of intent are confidential and will not be disclosed except to the parties' professional advisors

A statement that the seller will take the property off of the market and not accept other offers while a contract is being finalized (typically about a two week period).

After the letter of intent is completed and signed by both parties, the buyer typically has its lawyer prepare the formal purchase agreement, in accordance with the basic terms outlined in the letter of intent. It is the formal contract that sets forth the detail behind the generalities contained in the letter of intent. A one to two page letter of intent typically becomes a ten to twenty page purchase contract, depending upon the complexity of the deal.

At this point the distinction between brokers and lawyers should be examined. A broker is a deal finder and negotiator.

However, once the deal is found, your lawyer (preferably one who is skilled in real estate deals) should take over as the quarterback of your team. Remember that your broker only gets paid if the deal closes and the broker has no interest in performing the same work all over again because a deal fails. Your lawyer, on the other hand, is not compensated based on whether the deal closes. It is your lawyer's job to protect your interest, and to help you do the deal that you want to do.

It is also important to note that brokers often say that lawyers are not required and that they have standard form contracts that you can use (the pitch is that you don't need to waste money on a lawyer). While I generally agree that lawyers are not needed on residential transactions, lawyers are a must on commercial real estate transactions. Large transactions are typically too complex and too much is at stake not to employ counsel.

As to the "standard forms" utilized by brokers, they can work for simple deals. However, by law, brokers are prohibited from modifying those contracts to fit a particular scenario. In addition, in most states, the standardized forms are prepared by committees of lawyers and brokers. The typical result is a "middle of the road" contract that is as generic as possible and is more protective of the brokers than it is of the parties. When you are making your organizations largest investment, you need a contract that is drafted to fit your particular situation and, more importantly, is drafted with your interests in mind.

The key points that need to be covered in your purchase contract are as follows:

A correct identification of the parties to the contract and a legal description of the property to be sold. With the purchase and sale of churches and related properties, it is critical to describe in detail any non-realty items (such as furniture, sound equipment, television equipment and the like to be included in the sale. With the exception of items that are permanently affixed to the building, non-realty items are not assumed to be included in a sale unless they are specifically mentioned.

The contract needs to include the detail of the business points covered in the letter of intent.

The contract needs to be signed by persons authorized by each party to execute such contracts. It is important to note that your lawyer should review your organization's articles of incorporation and bylaws that determine who is authorized to sign contracts to buy/sell real estate and whether a board meeting or meeting of the members is required to authorize the purchase.

The contract needs to specify who is responsible for paying any real estate brokers and the amount that the brokers will be paid. It is advisable to have the broker sign the contract to evidence their agreement to the terms.

The contract needs to stipulate the amount of the earnest money deposit (also referred to in some areas as an escrow deposit) that the buyer will post when the contract is signed. The amount of the earnest money deposit is typically between one (1) and five (5) percent of the purchase price. The purpose of the deposit is to demonstrate the seriousness of the buyer.

The contract will specify under what circumstances the earnest money deposit is refundable. Most commercial real estate contracts provide that the buyer can terminate the contract, and receive a refund of the earnest money deposit, at any time during the due diligence period (also referred to as the feasibility period).

The reason for having a refundable earnest money deposit is a trade-off between buyers and sellers. Most sellers naturally want a nonrefundable deposit from the buyer. The sellers also want the sale to be "AS-IS, WHERE-IS" so that the seller is done with the property after the deal closes. The buyer, on the other hand, wants to know that the property is suitable and that the seller has good title to the property, before making an irrevocable commitment to buy, especially if the sale is "AS —IS." The result is a long-standing compromise that meets the most important needs of both parties. The earnest money deposit is put-up by the buyer and typically held by a title company. The deposit is fully refundable until the end of the due diligence or feasibility period. If the buyer has not terminated the contract by that time, the deposit becomes nonre-fundable or "goes hard." The buyer is protected because it has time to review the property before it makes an irrevocable decision to allow the money to go hard. At the same time, the seller knows to some degree at least, that the buyer is serious because the buyer put up significant money in escrow.

As a result of the foregoing, the buyer needs to have ample time to conduct its due diligence to insure that the property is suit-able for its needs. Due diligence is the series of tests, inspections and legal reviews that help you determine if the property meets your needs, that you will get good legal title to the property, and that there are no costly problems with the property (the steps are detailed below). Generally, it is very difficult to conduct a proper due diligence review in less than 60 days. Most experienced real estate sellers understand and will accommodate the need for a 60-90 day review. Beware the seller who insists on a very short time fuse, they are more likely than not hiding something and have a reason to complete the deal quickly.

The contract needs to specify the remedies that each party has if the other defaults on the deal. In other words, this section of the contract will list what your options are for recourse if the other side fails to complete the deal. The potential available remedies include everything from a lawsuit for damages or to force the seller to sell to a forfeiture or refund of the earnest money deposit. In order to avoid uncertainty, most savvy lawyers draft real estate contracts to eliminate the possibility of a lawsuit for money damages. Typically, most sellers are satisfied with a simple forfeiture of the earnest money deposit if the buyer defaults. This is a simple and easy remedy and is usually fair in terms of compensation of the seller for its loss (it still owns the property). A buyer typically wants to limit the seller's remedies to forfeiture because it eliminates the possibility of a lawsuit for damages (which can be costly).

In turn, most sellers typically want to limit the buyer's remedy for a seller default to a cancellation of the contract and a return of the deposit. However, this is unfair in two ways. First, the buyer (who is the one spending money on due diligence) simply has his or her own money refunded (and receives no compensation). Also, that arrangement makes it too easy for seller to cancel your deal to go with a better offer that comes along later. In order to solve that problem, one of two things is typically done. First, the buyer may retain the right to sue for specific performance. This is not a right to sue for money damages but is simply the right to sue to force the seller to complete the deal. In addition, the successful party in such a suit can typically recover attorney's fees (this becomes the leverage to force a defaulting seller to settle a valid lawsuit). Another alternative is to provide that the defaulting seller must reimburse the buyer for its out-of-pocket expenses, up to a cap. These options help insure that the buyer does not lose in the situation while, at the same time, protecting the parties from the uncertainty of a lawsuit for money damages.

The contract needs to specify that the seller will provide the buyer with a survey of the property and a commitment for title insurance. A survey is a drawing prepared by a licensed surveyor that shows the boundary of the property, the location of buildings on the property and any easements or rights of way that affect the property, and whether the property is in a flood zone. The title commitment shows who owns the property (hopefully your seller) and a description of any items that affect title to the property (such as liens, easements etc.). Typically, the seller pays for these items.

The contract should state when and where the transaction will be closed, what the parties must provide at the closing and who pays for what portion of the closing cost. While the division of expenses is the subject of local customs, it is typical for sellers to pay the cost of title insurance, survey, and the cost to prepare the deed. Buyers pay all costs associated with its loan and the Buyer and Seller equally share escrow fees. It is also standard that each party pays its own lawyers fees and that the seller pays the real estate brokers, if any. However, all of these cost points are negotiable and can provide a way to tweak the deal. Your lawyer should be able to estimate these expenses for you. Having the cost information will enable you to use that information to negotiate.

The contract needs to provide for certain disclosures and representations by the seller. The seller should disclose any known environmental problems with the property, whether there are any pending lawsuits involving the property and similar matters.

The contract should provide who has the risk of loss between contract signing and the closing. Typically, the contract will provide that the seller bears any risk of loss prior to the closing and will maintain casualty insurance until closing. Often, in the event of a casualty loss (such as a fire) the buyer will have the option of either (i) terminating the deal, (ii) requiring the seller to repair the property or (iii) taking the property as-is and having the seller turn over the insurance proceeds to the seller.

AGREEMENT OF SALE

The following is a sample purchase agreement for the acquisition of an existing church building and surrounding property. A review of this sample contract will illustrate the points made above.

THIS AGREEMENT OF SALE (this "Agreement") is made and entered into as of this 2nd day of August 2000 (the "Effective Date") by and between Selling Church, Inc. ("Seller") and Buying Church, Inc. ("Purchaser")

NOW, THEREFORE, for and in consideration of the mutual covenants and agreements herein contained and other good and valuable consideration, the receipt and sufficiency of which are hereby acknowledged, Seller and Purchaser hereby agree as follows:

Article I

Sale and Purchase of the Property

Agreement to Sell and Convey. Seller hereby agrees to sell and convey to Purchaser, and Purchaser hereby agrees to purchase from Seller, subject to the terms and conditions hereinafter set forth, all of the Property (hereinafter defined).

The term "Property" shall mean that certain tract of land situated in the City of Dallas, Dallas County, Texas, more particularly described on Exhibit "A" attached hereto and incorporated herein by reference, containing 25.25 acres, more or less, together with (i) all structures, fixtures and other improvements situated on such land, (ii) all sound equipment, furniture (including pews) and related items currently located in or used in connection with the operation of a church in the property, (iii) any and all rights, titles, powers, privileges, easements, licenses, rights-of-way and interests, if any, owned by Seller and appurtenant solely to such land and the foregoing described improvements, (iv) all rights, titles, powers, privileges, easements, licenses, rights-of-way and interests, if any, of Seller, either as law or in equity, in possession or in expectancy, in and to any real estate lying in the streets, highways, roads, alleys, rights-of-way or sidewalks, open or proposed, in front of, above, over, under, through or adjoining the land and in and to any strips or gores of real estate adjoining such land, and (v) all rights, titles, powers, privileges, easements, licenses, rights-of-way and interests, appurtenant or incident exclusively to any of the foregoing, if any.

Purchase Price. The purchase price (the "Purchase Price") to be paid for the

Property shall be payable at the Closing (hereinafter defined) by certified or cashier's check or wire transfer of immediately available funds ("Immediately Available Funds"), in an amount equal to Two Million and No/100 Dollars ($2,000,000.00).

Escrow Deposit.

For the purpose of securing the performance of Purchaser under the terms and provisions of this Agreement, Purchaser has, concurrently with the execution and delivery of this Agreement, delivered to Southwest Land Title Company (the "Title Company"), located at 1159 Cottonwood Lane, Suite 150, Irving, Texas 75038, Attention: Matt Anthony, an earnest money deposit in the amount of One Hundred Thousand and No/100 Dollars

($100,000.00), which shall be disbursed by the Title Company in accordance with the terms and provisions of this Agreement. Seller and Purchaser agree that One Hundred and No/100 Dollars ($100.00) of the amount deposited with the Title Company by Purchaser shall immediately become the property of Seller and is considered independent consideration paid by Purchaser (the "Independent Consideration"). The sum of One Hundred Thousand and No/100 Dollars ($100,000.00) deposited by Purchaser with the Title Company, less the Independent Consideration to Seller, is hereinafter referred to as the "Escrow Deposit." The Escrow Deposit shall be invested by the Title Company in a savings account or certificate of deposit as designated from time to time by Purchaser, and all interest earned with respect thereto shall be for the sole account of Deposit hereunder. All interest earned with respect to the Escrow Deposit shall be paid by the Title Company to Purchaser currently as it is earned. In the event that this Agreement is closed in accordance with the terms hereof, the Escrow Deposit shall be applied toward the cash payment due at the Closing by Purchaser to Seller. If Purchaser shall fail to deposit the Escrow Deposit within five (5) business days of the Effective Date, this Agreement shall automatically terminate.

By execution of this Agreement, the Title Company hereby agrees to act as escrow agent and disburse the Escrow Deposit in accordance with the terms and provisions of this Agreement.

Feasibility Period. Purchaser shall have until 5:00 p.m. on the sixtieth (60th) day after the Effective Date (the "Feasibility Period") to make all inspections, studies and investigations desired by Purchaser with respect to the Property, including, without limitation, an environmental assessment study and soil tests. Purchaser and its authorized agents and representatives shall be entitled to enter upon the Property at all reasonable times prior to the expiration of Feasibility Period for the purpose of conducting any and all inspections, studies and investigations which Purchaser deems advisable. Purchaser shall restore the Property to as near the same condition as it existed immediately upon the completion thereof. Purchaser shall indemnify, defend and hold Seller and the Property harmless of and from any and all losses, liabilities, costs and expenses arising from or related to Purchaser's tests, studies, investigations or inspections of the Property.

Purchaser's indemnification obligations shall survive the Closing or earlier termination of this Agreement. Seller shall furnish to Purchaser within five (5) days after the Effective Date all engineering plans, drawings, surveys, artists' renderings, and economic and financial studies which Seller may have relating to the Property. Purchaser shall keep the information contained in any and all materials delivered to Purchaser strictly confidential, shall use such information for internal purposes only, and shall return any and all such materials delivered to Purchaser by Seller to Seller, at its request, if this Agreement is terminated by either party for any reason or if the Closing of the sale contemplated hereby is not consummated. However, notwithstanding anything contained herein to the contrary, Purchaser may disclose any information contained in any materials delivered to Purchaser to Purchaser to Purchaser's attorneys, accountants, management company, consultants, advisors, any prospective tenant or user of the Property, and any third party lender with the instructions from Purchaser that such recipients of the information are to keep the information confidential. If, prior to the expiration of the Feasibility Period, Purchaser fails to give written notice to Seller of its acceptance of the Property and deliver an additional Escrow Deposit (the

"Additional Escrow Deposit") in the amount of Seventy-five Thousand and No/100 Dollars ($75,000.00) to the Title Company, this Agreement shall automatically terminate without further action by either party hereto, and the Initial Escrow Deposit shall be immediately refunded to Purchaser by the Title Company, and neither party shall have any further right or obligation hereunder except for the provisions hereof which expressly survive the termination of this Agreement. If Purchaser does accept the Property and delivers the Additional Escrow Deposit to the Title Company, both the Initial Escrow Deposit and the Additional Escrow Deposit shall become non-refundable, but shall be applied to the Purchase Price at closing.

Article II

Survey and Title Commitment; Permitted Exceptions

Review of Preliminary Title Report and Survey. Within ten (10) days after

the Effective Date, Seller, at Seller's sole cost and expense, shall cause the Title Company to issue and deliver to Purchaser a title commitment (the "Title Commitment") showing the status of title to the Property issued by the Title Company, accompanied by one (1) legible copy of all documents referred to in the Title Commitment (the "Exception Documents"). Purchaser shall give Seller written notice on or before the expiration of thirty (30) days after the last to be received of the Title Commitment, the Exception Documents and the Survey (hereinafter defined) that the condition of title as set forth in the Title Commitment and the Survey and the content of the Title Commitment and the Survey are or are not satisfactory. In the event Purchaser states that the condition of title or the content of the Title Commitment and Survey are not satisfactory, Seller shall use reasonable good faith efforts to cure (and will cooperate with Purchaser to cure), eliminate or modify all such unacceptable matters to the satisfaction of Purchaser, in Purchaser's reasonable discretion, but in no event whatsoever shall Seller be obligated to pay to any third party any fees, costs or expenses regarding the cure of any of Purchaser's objections. In the event Seller is unable or unwilling to satisfy Purchaser's objections prior to the expiration of the Feasibility Period, Purchaser may, at its option, terminate this Agreement. If Purchaser does not terminate this Agreement within such period (or fails to give notice to Seller of any objections to the Title Commitment or the Survey within thirty (30) days after the last to be received of the Title Commitment, the Exception Documents and the Survey), Purchaser shall have waived its rights to do so, and shall be deemed to have accepted to have accepted title, the Title Commitment and the Survey subject to the objections raised by Purchaser (or failed to be raised), without an adjustment in the Purchase Price. If Purchaser terminates this Agreement, the Escrow Deposit shall be immediately returned to Purchaser by the Title Company and neither party shall have any further right or obligation hereunder except for the provisions hereof which expressly survive the termination of this Agreement.

Current Survey. Seller, at Seller's sole cost and expense, shall, within ten (10) days after the Effective Date, deliver to Purchaser and the Title Company a current survey of the Property, prepared by a registered and licensed land surveyor acceptable to Purchaser and the Title Company (the "Survey"). The Survey shall:

Set forth an accurate metes and bounds description of the Property;Locate all existing improvements, building and setback lines, fences, evidence of abandoned fences, easements and rights-of-way (setting forth the book and page number of the recorded instruments creating the same), alleys, streets and roads, and all land lying within any flood prone area or any area within the 100-year flood plan;

Show all encroachments upon the Property; Contain a surveyor's certification in form and containing substance reasonably acceptable to Purchaser and the Title Company; Show all dedicated public and all private streets providing access to the Property and whether such access is paved to the property line of the Property; and (f) Substantially conform to the requirements of Category 1A, Condition II Land Title Survey of the Texas Society of Professional Surveyors Standards and Specifications.

Seller hereby agrees, at its own reasonable cost and expense, to cause such additional surveying work to be timely completed as may be reasonably necessary or required by the Title Company for its issuance of the Title Policy (hereinafter defined).

Permitted Encumbrance. The Property shall be conveyed to Purchaser subject to no liens, charges, encumbrances, exceptions, or reservations of any kind or character other than the easements, exceptions and other encumbrances, if any, described on Schedule B of the Title Commitment as approved by Purchaser or deemed approved, provided that (i) the exception as to rights of parties in possession shall be deleted, and (ii) the exception relating to taxes shall be limited to standby fees, taxes and assessments by any taxing authority for the year 2001, and subsequent years, and subsequent taxes and assessments by any taxing authority for prior years due to change in land usage or ownership (collectively, the "Permitted Encumbrances").

Article III

Provisions With Respect to Closing

Closing Date. The consummation of the transactions contemplated by this Agreement (the "Closing") shall take place in the offices of the Title Company, on or before September 15, 2000 (the "Closing Date").Seller's Obligations at Closing. At the Closing, Seller shall execute, acknowledge (where appropriate) and deliver to Purchaser (and in the case of clause (d), the Title company), at Seller's sole cost and expense, the following: a Special Warranty Deed conveying the Property to Purchaser subject only to the Permitted Encumbrances; an owner's title insurance policy issued by the Title Company (the "Title Policy"), insuring good and indefeasible fee simple title to the Property in Purchaser in a face amount equal to the Purchase Price, and containing no exceptions other than the Permitted Encumbrances; provided that Seller will, at its expense, cause the Title Company to modify the Title Policy to (i) except only for standby fees, taxes and assessments by any taxing authority for the year 2001, and subsequent years, and subsequent taxes and assessments by any taxing authority for prior years due to change in land usage or ownership; and (ii) delete the exception as to rights of parties in possession; a certificate stating that Seller is not a "foreign person" as required by Section 1145 of the Internal Revenue Code of 1986, as amended; andsuch other instruments and documents (including, without limitation, evidence of Seller's legal capacity and authority to enter into this Agreement, a closing statement and Seller's affidavit), as are reasonably required by the Title Company to consummate the transaction contemplated hereby.Purchaser's Obligations at Closing. At the Closing, Purchaser shall, at Purchaser's sole cost and expense, do the following:deliver to the Title Company, in Immediately Available Funds, an amount equal to the Purchase Price less the amount of the Escrow Deposit and the prorations payable by Seller, and thereupon authorize the Title Company to deliver such funds to Seller; andExecute and deliver to the Title Company such instruments and documents (including, without limitation, evidence of Purchaser's legal capacity and authority to enter into this Agreement and a closing statement) as are reasonably required by the Title Company to consummate the transaction contemplated hereby.

Closing Costs. Seller shall pay the cost of that preparation and recording of the Special Warranty Deed and the premiums for the Title Policy to be furnished to Purchaser at the Closing. The escrow fees of the Title Company shall be shared equally by Seller and Purchaser. Any other costs of Closing shall be paid by the party for whom it is customary in normal commercial real estate transactions in Dallas County, Texas to pay. Each party shall pay its own attorneys' fees.

Payment and Proration of Taxes and Assessments. Ad valorem taxes for the year of the Closing shall be prorated to the date of Closing. If the Closing shall occur before the tax rate is fixed for the then current year, the apportionment of taxes shall be upon the basis of the tax rate for the preceding year applied to the latest assessed valuation. Subsequent to the Closing, when the tax rate is fixed for the year in which the Closing occurs, Seller and Purchaser agree to adjust the proration of taxes and, if necessary, to refund or pay (as the case may be) such sums shall be necessary to effect such adjustment. All taxes assessed because of a change of use or ownership of the Property on or after the Closing related to the period of time prior to the Closing shall be assumed and paid by Seller and Seller shall indemnify, defend and hold Purchaser harmless from any and all losses, liabilities, costs and expenses arising from such taxes. The obligations set forth in this Section 3.5 shall survive the Closing of this Agreement.

Article IV

Representations and Warranties With Respect to the Property Seller represents and warrants to Purchaser as follows:

4.1 Indefeasible Title. At the Closing, Seller will have good, and indefeasible title to the Property.

No Condemnation Pending or Threatened. No notice of any pending condemnation proceeding has been received, and to Seller's current, actual knowledge, there are no threatened or contemplated condemnation or similar proceeding affecting the Property or any portion thereof. Pending Litigation. Seller has received no notice of any legal actions, suits, or other legal administrative proceedings, pending or to Seller's current actual knowledge, threatened, against or affecting the Property. Authority. Seller has, or will have at Closing, the full right, power, and authority to sell and convey the Property as provided in this Agreement and to carry out Seller's obligations hereunder, and that all requisite action necessary to authorize Seller to enter into this Agreement and to carry out Seller's obligations hereunder has been, or on the Closing Date will have bee, taken.

No Other Contracts. Seller has not entered into any contracts for the sale of the Property which are still in effect and neither any tenant nor any other person or entity has any rights of first refusal, option or other preferential right to purchase the Property.

The representations, warranties and covenants set forth in this Article IV shall be continuing and shall be true and correct on and as of the Closing Date with the same force and effect as if made at that time, and all of such representations, warranties and covenants shall survive the Closing for a period of nine (9) months and shall not be affected by any investigation, verification, or approval by any party hereto or by anyone on behalf of any party hereto.

Article V

Provisions With Respect to Default

Default by Seller. In the event that Seller should default in its obligations herein for any reason whatsoever, except Purchaser's default, or if any of Seller's representations and warranties contained herein shall not be true and correct in all material respects, Purchaser may as Purchaser's sole and exclusive remedy, either (i) enforce specific performance of this Agreement or (ii) terminate this Agreement, whereupon the Escrow Deposit shall be immediately returned to Purchaser by the Title Company.

Default by Purchaser. In the event Purchaser should default in its obligations to purchase the Property hereunder for any reason, except a default by Seller or the termination by Purchaser of this Agreement pursuant to a right of termination granted herein or as the result of the non-satisfaction of any conditions to Purchaser's obligations hereunder, Seller as its sole and exclusive remedy shall receive the Escrow Deposit from the Title Company as liquidated damages; Purchaser and Seller hereby agree that actual damages would be difficult or impossible to ascertain and such amount is a reasonable estimate of the damages for such breach.

Article VI

Miscellaneous

Brokerage Fees and Commissions. John A. Broker ("Broker") represents the Seller. Seller agrees to pay Brokers the fee specified by separate agreement between Broker and Seller. Broker agrees to pay Hardesty Realty Group ("Co-Broker"), on, but only upon, closing of the purchase and sale contemplated by this Agreement, a fee of, one-half of the fee payable to Broker, if , as and when the purchase and sale is closed. Seller, Broker, Co-Broker and Purchaser hereby acknowledge and agree that Purchaser has no liability, obligation or responsibility to pay Broker or Co-Broker a fee or commission. It is agreed that, except as set forth above, if any claims for brokerage commissions or fees are ever made against Seller or Purchaser in connection with this transaction, all such claims shall be handled and paid by the party whose commitments form the basis of such claim. It is further agreed that each party agrees to indemnify and hold harmless the other from and against any and all such claims or demands with respect to any brokerage fees or agents' commissions or other compensation asserted by any person, firm, or corporation in connection with this Agreement or the transactions contemplated hereby insofar as any such claim or demand is based upon a contract or commitment of the indemnifying party.

Notices. Any notice to be given or to be served upon any party hereto in connection with this Agreement must be in writing, and shall be deemed, given and received (i) two (2) days after being sent by United States certified or registered mail, return receipt requested, properly addressed, with postage prepaid, (ii) when delivered to and received by the party to whom it is addressed with respect to personal delivery, (iii) one (1) day after being deposited with a nationally recognized overnight courier service, charges prepaid, properly addressed, or (iv) upon receipt of a confirmation of

transmission to the proper number when sent by facsimile properly addressed. Such notices shall be given to the parties hereto at
the following addresses;

If to Seller:

Selling Church, Inc.

1400 Post Oak Blvd.

Suite 400

Dallas, TX 75231

Telephone: _____

Fax: _____

If to Purchaser

Buying Church, Inc.

5787 S. Hampton Rd

Suite 445, LB 125

Dallas, TX 75232

Telephone: (214-337-4100)

Fax: (214-337-4455)

Any party hereto may, at any time by giving written notice to
the other party hereto in accordance with the terms of this paragraph, designate any other address or facsimile number in substitu-
tion of the foregoing address to which such notice shall be given.

Entire Agreement: Modification. This Agreement embodies

and constitutes the entire understanding among the parties with respect to the transactions contemplated herein, and all prior or contemporaneous agreements, understandings, representation and statements, oral or written, are merged into this Agreement. Neither this Agreement nor any provision hereof may be waived, modified, amended, discharged or terminated except by an instrument in writing signed by the party against which the enforcements of such waiver, modification, amendment, discharge or termination is sought, and then only to the extent set forth in such instrument.

Headings. Descriptive headings are for convenience only and shall notcontrol or affect the meaning or construction of any provision of this Agreement.

Attorney's Fees. If either party shall initiate legal proceedings to enforce itsrights hereunder, the nonprevailing party shall pay the reasonable attorneys' fees incurred by the prevailing party.

Execution by Seller. This Agreement may be executed in counterparts, each of which shall constitute an original, and all of which, taken together, shall constitute a single Agreement.

Business Days. If the final date of any period falls upon a Saturday, Sundayor legal holiday under the laws of the State of Texas, then in such event the time of such period shall be extended to the next day which is not a Saturday, Sunday or legal holiday under the laws of the State of Texas.

Assignment. This Agreement may be assigned by Purchaser in whole or in part without the consent of Seller.

Choice of Law. This Agreement shall be construed under and in accordance with the laws of the State of Texas, and all obligations of the parties created hereunder are performable in Dallas County, Texas.

Binding on Successors and Assigns. This Agreement shall be binding upon and inure to the benefit of the parties hereto, their respective heirs, executors, administrators, legal representatives, successors, and permitted assigns.

Severability. In case any one or more of the provisions contained in this Agreement shall for any reason be held to be invalid, illegal, or unenforceable in any respect, such invalidity, illegality, or unenforceability shall not affect any other provision hereof, and this Agreement shall be construed as if such invalid, illegal, or unenforceable provision had never been contained herein. Furthermore, in lieu of any such invalid, illegal or unenforceable provision, there shall be automatically added to this Agreement a provision as similar to such illegal, invalid or unenforceable provision as may be possible and be legal, valid and enforceable.

Time of Essence. This is of the essence with this Agreement.

Gender, etc. Words of any gender used in this Agreement shall be held and construed to include any other gender, and words in the singular number shall be held to include the plural, and vice versa, unless the context requires otherwise.

Counterparts. The parties may execute this Agreement in one or more identical counterparts, all of which when taken together will constitute one and the same instrument.

IN WITNESS WHEREOF, the parties hereto have executed this Agreement as of the Effective Date.

PURCHASER:

Buying Church, inc.

By: _____

Name: _____

Title: _____

SELLER:

SELLING CHURCH, INC.

By: _____

Name: _____

Title: _____

ACCEPTANCE BY THE TITLE COMPANY

Southwest Land Title Company hereby acknowledged receipt of the Escrow Deposit referred to in the foregoing Agreement of Sale and agrees to accept, hold, and return such Escrow Deposit and to immediately disburse any funds received thereunder, in accordance with the provisions of such Agreement of Sale without the necessity of any further release, authorization or direction from either Seller or Purchaser.

SOUTHWEST LAND TITLE COMPANY

By: _____

Name: _____

Title: _____

DUE DILIGENCE INVESTIGATION

After the contract is signed, the buyer should immediately begin its due diligence investigation. By the time you select the property and negotiate a price, you know that the building will meet your basic needs and objectives. The goal of the due diligence investigation (or feasibility study) is to look very closely and see if there are any hidden problems that will negatively impact the value of the property. For instance, you need to be sure the property is structurally sound and that the major systems work. Second, you need to be sure that there are no legal problems with the property, such as title or environmental issues.

It is very important that the due diligence be coordinated by your lawyer. Having your lawyer drive this process will provide your lawyer with the full picture concerning the property and enable him or her to act accordingly. For instance, discovery of an environmental problem will impact how you proceed under your contract and, therefore, your lawyer should be involved. Moreover, good real estate lawyers frequently oversee such investigations and know what to look for with certain types of properties.

Generally, the due diligence investigation should cover the following steps:

1. Title and Survey Review

Your lawyer will order and obtain a title commitment and a survey. A title commitment is a document provided by a title insurance company. By issuing a title commitment, the title company promises to issue you at closing and upon payment of the quoted premium, a title insurance policy guaranteeing that your church receives good title to the property, subject only to the exceptions listed on the title commitment. The title company then provides your attorney with a copy of all of the official documents that are referenced in the title commitment.

Your lawyer will review the title commitment, along with the supporting documents provided by the title company, and inform you as to the state of title to the property. Every title commitment will list numerous exceptions to the title insurance, these are items that affect, in some way, the ownership of the property. Your lawyer's job is to determine if any of the listed items will affect your use of the property.

For example, the exceptions may include the fact that an oil company holds mineral rights to the property and can, if it chooses, place a well on the property. If the oil company in fact has the right to and chooses to drill, your use of the property would be greatly impacted. As a buyer, you need to understand this risk.

In addition, all liens against the property will be listed on the title commitment. Your lawyer will need to make sure that all of those liens are released prior to closing.

Part of the lawyer's job, as well, is to make sure that the title company drafts its exceptions as clearly and as narrowly as possible. The title company should only except to items that clearly impact title to the specific property. Specificity is needed in the event that the title company misses something and you later need to make a claim under the policy. If the commitment and issued policy contain broad sweeping exceptions, it gives the title company wiggle room to try to avoid a valid claim at a later date.

Along with the title commitment, your lawyer will obtain and review a title survey of the property. A title survey is a drawing, prepared by a licensed surveyor, that shows the boundaries of the property, the locations of buildings on the property and the dimensions and locations of any items that affect the property. For instance, the survey should reveal if building encroaches onto a neighbor's property or if part of the property is in the flood plain.

It is important that your lawyer review the survey in conjunction with the title commitment. For instance, it is very likely that the title commitment will show that the electric company has an easement on a part of your property for the purpose of placing electrical lines on the property. Such an easement is common and, in fact, necessary so that the electric company can get its lines to your property. So, by itself, the title commitment will normally reveal nothing out of the ordinary. However, the survey should show the exact location of the easement. It may be that the electric company has an easement that goes under your building. In such a case, your lawyer would need to work with the seller and the electric company to see if the location of the easement can be changed so that you do not later have to deal with the electric company trying to bulldoze your building to put a new line in place.

As part of the due diligence process, I highly suggest that you request that your lawyer provide you with a detailed memorandum detailing the results of his or her title and survey review. This way, you will be sure what types of items impact the property.

As discussed, the title and survey review that your lawyer will undertake is really a precursor to obtaining proper title insurance at the closing. Title insurance is really a simple concept. The title insurance company is insuring that you will, in fact, own the property after closing and that your ownership and use of the property will be absolute except for the items excepted to in the policy. At its most basic level, this means that if someone shows up later and claims they, not you, own the property, you can make a claim under your title insurance policy. At that point, the title company will defend you against the claim by the other party and, if you lose, the title company will pay you the amount specified under the policy.

Here is an example of a real case that I worked on for a church. The church had purchased a tract of raw land where they planned to build a church. After raising funds, the church started construction and in the process of excavating the site the contractor discovered a large drainage pipe running through the center of the property.

After an investigation, it was discovered that the State Highway Department did, in fact, have a valid drainage easement through the property. The easement document prohibited the construction of any building over any part of the easement (this is typical of utility, pipeline, or drainage easements because the company placing the lines on the property may need to dig them up to repair them at some point). However, both the title company and the surveyor simply missed the easement when they conducted their title searches. As a result, the easement was not listed on the title commitment or policy and was not shown on the survey. The end result was that the title company paid the church's claim. Without title insurance, the church would have been holding the bag on a property it could not use.

2. Zoning Verification

The zoning of the property will need to be verified to clarify that you can use the property for all of the uses that you have in mind. This is easily done by requesting a zoning verification letter from the city zoning department and getting a copy of the city code listing the requirements and permitted uses for the specific zoning designation that applies to your property.

If you are buying an existing church building, it is unlikely that a zoning issue will arise impacting the right to conduct church on the site. However, the zoning of the property may well impact other, non-church, uses such as a retirement home, housing, or a school. Because the issue of zoning has a far greater impact in the process of building a new facility, the issue will be more fully discussed under the section on new church construction.

3. Environmental Site Assessment

One the most important steps that you need to take is to retain an environmental testing firm to conduct what is known as a Phase One environmental site assessment of the property. This assessment is a preliminary investigation that determines only whether there is reason to believe that environmental contamination is present on the property. The testing firm examines the property and its historical uses (was there a factory or a gas station on the property or was it built during the time period when asbestos or other hazardous materials were widely used). In addition, the environmental clean-up databases are searched to determine if any of the property is in an area known to have been contaminated.

Based on the data, a judgment is made as to the likelihood of contamination being present. If the likelihood is very low, the testing firm will find that no further testing is required. Accordingly, your receipt of a clean Phase One Environmental Site Assessment does not guarantee that no contamination exists on the property that you are buying. It just means that no reason exists to look further.

While such a result is not an absolute guarantee, it has several benefits. First a Phase One Site Assessment costs a fraction of the amount of a Phase Two Site Assessment (which involves actual soil and materials testing in a lab). Second, the fact that you obtained a clean Phase One makes you an innocent purchaser if later contamination is found. While your status as an innocent purchaser does not completely remove any responsibility you have (because you do own the property and will need to resolve the contamination in order to be able to sell the property), it will provide some protection against legal action by the government. Generally, the government is very favorably inclined to work with innocent landowners. For instance, the government may aid your efforts to pursue the actual wrongdoers and may even make clean up funds available to you.

Another very important reason exists for obtaining the Phase One. A clean Phase One will protect all of your officers and directors from any personal liability for clean up costs. In the case of environmental contamination, the government has the ability to pierce the corporate shield and pursue individual officers and directors of non-profit corporations, if those officers and directors were involved in purchasing contaminated property without having first obtained a Phase One report.

In the event that the Phase One report finds that contamination is possible and that further testing is warranted, a Phase Two Site Assessment is recommended. A Phase Two involves actual testing of materials and soil samples to verify the presence or absence of actual contaminants. A clean Phase Two provides the same benefits as a clean Phase One.

It should be noted that virtually all lenders will require that you perform a Phase One before they will make a loan on a property. The reason is very simple. If a bank makes a loan on a property, it is possible that the bank might foreclose on that property one day and, as a result, the bank wants to know if it could be inheriting a costly environmental problem.

One final note, if the property you want does, in fact, have some contamination problem, all hope is not lost. The local, state, and federal governments all have programs designed to help innocent landowners rehabilitate environmentally damaged properties. Known as "brownfields" programs, these programs make funds and expertise available to help landowners who want to clean up someone else's mess.

Moreover, everything is negotiable. The sellers of environmentally contaminated property are often extremely motivated sellers. As a result, if you clearly understand the problem, clearly understand the cost of fixing the problem, and clearly understand the resources available to you, it may be possible to make a great deal. However, if you did not do your homework up-front, you will find yourself with a massive problem. Accordingly, if you proceed to acquire a contaminated property, be very careful and obtain a lawyer who does nothing but handle environmental problems.

A quick story will illustrate the potential difficulties in dealing with environmental matters. A church that I represented owned a vacant lot adjacent to the church. The plan was to eventually build a football field on the lot for the church's private school. One day, a dump truck driver saw the vacant lot and asked if the church would like fill dirt to level the lot. Someone at the church thought it was a great idea. Over the next few days, over fifty dump trucks deposited dirt on the vacant lot.

Later on, the problem was discovered. The dirt was from the excavation of an auto repair facility and was contaminated with various petroleum products, such as used motor oil, gasoline and the like. The church had done nothing wrong, but the ensuing dispute took over a year to resolve. While the responsible party ultimately cleaned-up the problem, the church still paid out thousands in legal fees and environmental testing fees before the people who dumped the dirt would accept responsibility and resolve it. Moreover, later efforts to refinance the church became problematic because this past environmental problem had to be disclosed and explained to the bank and further testing had to be done to prove to the bank that no problem existed. The point is that environmental problems can arise in a myriad of ways. Anything that can impact the environmental condition of the property should be dealt with carefully

3.Engineering Review

Early on, an engineering firm needs to be retained to evaluate the structural integrity of the building and whether the various systems, such as HVAC, electrical and plumbing systems are in working order. Typically, commercial buildings are purchased on an as-is basis, without any guarantee. Therefore, it is crucial to know what you are buying.

Far too often, churches buy a building based on a walk-through by the pastor or a member of the church who is in the construction business. It is that type of an attempt to save a few dollars that inevitably ends up costing a church thousands, if not hundreds of thousands of dollars later on because readily apparent problems were not spotted.

In addition, this review should consider whether the building meets current building codes. When the ownership of a building changes, you are typically required to obtain a new certificate of occupancy from the local building official. Many local building officials take advantage of ownership changes to force up-grades in buildings. Therefore, even if everything is in working order, you need to know if you will be able to obtain a new certificate of occupancy without significant upgrades to the building.

At this juncture, I want to emphasize an important point. It is often a bad idea to rely on and do business with church members. Particularly in real estate transactions where the stakes are very high, you need to know that you are getting the best possible guidance and advice. While your members will try to help, it is true virtually without exception, that professionals who are not being paid will not perform at the same level as professionals who are being paid to perform the job. Everyone has to make a living and, out of necessity, the jobs that professionals do as a favor take a backseat to paying jobs.

Even if the church member is in the business of doing what you have paid him to do and you are paying him, you have a problem if a dispute arises. It is one thing to terminate a third-party professional who is not performing, it is something else to fire a long-time dedicated tithe paying member who may have influence with other members of your church. The potential upside of working with a known and trusted church member is simply not worth the potential headache.

At the conclusion of the due diligence investigation, you should review all of the due diligence findings with your lawyer and broker. At this point, a decision needs to be made based on the available information: is the building suitable for your church's needs and is it a good deal. If the answer to both questions is yes, continue forward and close the purchase. If it is not suitable, terminate the deal and start looking for another deal. If the building works, but new information reveals that you may not be making a good business deal (you just found out that the building needs $100,000 in repairs), then you need to re-negotiate your deal based on the new information.

As you go through the buying process, you must maintain your ability to negotiate. That means that your purchase contract must give you ample time to conduct your due diligence and back-out if you find problems. It also means that you need to remain non-committal in terms of announcements to your congregation. For fundraising purposes, the pastor of the buying church often wants to make a big announcement as soon as, and often before, the contract is signed. The problem is that you become hamstrung and lose your negotiating ability once the entire congregation has locked into one property. If the sellers find out that you cannot back out, you have lost your biggest edge — the ability to walk away. Therefore, you need to get your congregation excited about buying a new building, but be circumspect until everything is done.

The remaining steps in buying an existing building are obtaining your financing and then actually closing the deal. The options for financing are discussed below in the section on church financing. As for the actual closing, it can be an experience unto itself. If all goes well and your advisors, particularly your lawyer, has done his job well and everything lines up properly, the closing can be a simple twenty-minute procedure of signing a very large stack of legal documents. More often, a real estate closing can be an often rescheduled, drawn-out affair. A real estate deal has a hundred moving parts and requires a large number of people, including appraisers, surveyors, engineers, lawyers, bankers, title examiners, buyers, and sellers to be coordinated and do their jobs and have everything ready to go at the same time. Such coordination can be a difficult thing to achieve.

One important point for the closing, even if you have counsel and an excellent team of advisors, I urge you to read the documents before the closing. Go over the documents with your lawyer and make sure that you understand the meaning of the documents and what your obligations are. To help you get started, the following is a partial listing of many of the pertinent documents a buyer will see or be asked to sign at the closing:

Post-Closing Matters

Following the closing, four important matters need to taken care of. Make sure that you receive an original title insurance policy from the title company. This should be done within two weeks of closing, at the latest. Make sure that you receive the original record-ed deed.

Someone (usually your lawyer) should make sure that you receive a binder including copies of each and every document signed at the closing. Keep all of these documents together in a safe place and make sure your attorney keeps copies at his or her office also.

Apply for a property tax exemption on the property. Churches are not automatically exempt from property taxes and are often sur-prised when they receive notice of taxes due. The exemption has to be applied for and granted. Even if you buy an exempt property, the tax assessor will remove the property from the list of exempted prop-erties as soon as the assessor sees that the property has been sold.

The exemption process is usually very simple and can be taken care of very quickly. However, skipping this step can result in an unnecessary tax bill because a deadline was missed (most tax author-ities require exemptions to be filed by a certain time each year).

New Church Construction

The alternative to buying an existing building is the construc-tion of a new facility. Without a doubt, construction of a new facil-ity, particularly on a new site, is one of the most complex and expensive undertakings a church can ever embark upon. This long, complex process will likely strain the Church's financial and per-sonnel resources; causing considerable stress for the leadership as well as the congregation of the Church.

The source of the strain is readily apparent. The process requires a Pastor and his or her staff to deal with a myriad of experts in diverse fields from lawyers, real estate brokers and owners, bankers, contractors, architects, to engineers and city government officials. To make matters worse, far to many unscrupulous characters have found their way into this business.

While no single chapter can address all of the issues involved in the church construction process, this chapter attempts to highlight a few points to keep in mind. The major steps in a construction project are as follows:

The Big Questions

The big questions are what do you want and need and what can your congregation afford. The question of affordability is addressed above and does not need to be dealt with again in any detail. However, one note needs to be added to the affordability equation when new construction is contemplated. Leave yourself plenty of room for added expenses and changes. You need to carry a hefty contingency budget line item throughout the entire process. It is inevitable that changes will be made to your plans as you progress, some will be major, some will be minor, and all will cost money. In addition, market changes over the 12-18 months it take to complete a project will result in price and cost changes. For instance, the price of lumber or concrete can vary greatly within a year's time. Likewise interest rates on your loan can move significantly over several months. The bottom-line is be prepared for unexpected expenses.

The next question is much more difficult. The easy part of the equation is based upon the number, type, and configuration of seats desired. An experienced architect can make rough estimates of required building size and city mandated parking requirements based on the number of desired seats. However, the real answers must be based upon an analysis of the church's programming needs. For example, the need for office and educational space will impact building size. Similarly, whether you plan only one service or multiple services will impact parking needs because a 3500 seat church with two Sunday services will, as a practical matter, need much more parking than a 3500 seat church with one service (even though the additional parking will generally not be required by the city). Also, audio/visual needs and expectations can greatly impact both building design and final cost.

After a rough building size and parking requirements are determined, you can roughly determine your requirements for a land purchase by adding the land area required for your building pad, parking, open space and (very important) future growth. In most cases, you should buy more land than you think you will ever need. Too often, churches get boxed in because of a lack of land and are forced to make a costly relocation because they cannot expand on their current site.

As you begin the process of making initial decisions and planning your project, I cannot emphasize enough the need to begin assembling the core components of your construction team as soon as possible. Putting the team together before any significant decisions are made to purchase land or set a building budget or other significant matters, will likely save you some real money. The process of developing a church campus involves hundreds of interrelated decisions, each one affecting scores of other decisions. The keys to success are a clear strategy and a qualified team of professionals. Anytime you have to back-track because you obtained information after a decision was made, will cost real money and time.

The group that you assemble will eventually consist of the following team members:

a.The team leader — This person should be the church's representative on the team. This person, above all, needs to be a manager and needs to be empowered by the church to guide the process. More than a construction expert, this person needs to be skilled in managing people and managing budgets. In other words, you need a skilled businessperson. The position will be very time consuming, especially at the outset of the process, and I advise against having the pastor as the team leader.

First, with all due respect, with the exception of a very few, most pastors are not businesspeople. Moreover, most pastors cannot devote the necessary time to the project. Finally, this person needs to be able to kick butts from time to time and that can be a very difficult thing for a pastor who has to worry about image. Accordingly, I suggest that you select the best businessperson on your staff to lead the project.

Construction Manager — Even though a church staff member is leading the project, you should strongly consider adding a well-qualified construction manager to your team. There are three major elements of your team, the church, the contractor, and the architect. Both the chosen contractor and architect will be professional in their field. Your staff member most likely will not be a professional in the construction business and, as a result, will be at a significant disadvantage when dealing with the contractor and architect. Moreover the contractor and architect each have their own interest to look after and, despite what they say, will not be looking out for you as much as they look out for themselves. That means that you need someone looking out for you and only you as you move through this process.

Bringing on a construction manager is really a matter of accountability. The manager's job is to maintain accountability in the process. You have three overriding issues in any construction project. You want the job done correctly, you want the job done on time, and you want the job done on budget. The construction manager's job is to keep the contractor and architect accountable in all three areas.

The selection of the construction manager is probably the single most important decision you will make in this process and it is also the first decision that you should make. I recommend that you interview a number of firms and look very closely at their experience with similar projects and talk extensively with references. In addition, you need to insist on individually interviewing the specific individual who will be responsible for your project on a day to day basis (this should be done with the contractor and architect as well). You will live with this individual for at least 18 months and will need to have trust and a good working relationship with this person. It does not matter how great the firm is that you hired if you cannot work with the person they assign to your project.

c.Contractor —The general contractor that you select will oversee the actual construction of your building. They generally will not do the actual work. Instead, they will hire and coordinate the actual sub-contractors that will do the work. When selecting the contractor, you are going to be primarily concerned about fees and the quality of work that will be performed on your behalf.

At this point, it should be noted that contractors are selected in two ways. In some cases, you hire a construction manager and an architect, have plans drawn and put the plans out to bid. In that case, you will select several qualified contractors and ask them to quote a price to build a building in accordance with the plans and specifications that the architect has drawn.

This two-step process has pros and cons. The pro is that you can get a set guaranteed price from a contractor before construction starts. The downside is that this process takes a long time. In addition, you do not have any idea what the building that your architect is drawing will cost to build until you get the bids. If you choose this route, and do so without the benefit of a construction manager, you will have an architect-controlled project. The risk is that you spend hundreds of thousands of dollars on plans you may not be able to use.

For example, I was once hired by a church after they found out that the plans drawn by the architect would cost $11,000,000 to build and the church had a $7,000,000 budget. Remember, architects are, in part, artists and great architects will design great buildings, but often without thought of practicality or budgets. It is the construction manager's job to provide the balance and accountability that you need.

The second way to hire a contractor is early on in the process. Once you, your construction manager, and possibly your architect have created a concept of the type of building that you want and have a rough budget in place, a list of qualified contractors can be selected to make proposals. In this instance, the contractors will not be bidding on a specific set of plans, but instead will propose to construct the building for actual cost, plus a negotiated fee. Most experienced contractors will likely propose relatively similar fee structures. As a result, in this scenario, you will be selecting the contractor based primarily on reputation and on the strength of the individuals who will be assigned to the project.

The benefit of this approach is speed. The project can proceed while plans are being drawn and projects can move much faster. In addition, if the effort is well coordinated, money can be saved because all of the parties — the church, the construction manager, and the architect work together to design the building. The contractor or construction manager will often be able to point out cost saving options to the church and architect as the plans proceed.

d.Architect—This is the firm that will design the building that you will occupy. The architect has to blend art and practicality and function together to create a functional space that hopefully also has an element of beauty that will make you happy to call the finished product home for years to come.

When selecting an architect, look closely at their past work. Do they have experience designing the type of building that you want. For instance, if your church is performance oriented, does the architect have experience designing performance spaces.

As with the contractor, you will ultimately select the architect based on experience, fees, and the quality of the individuals who will do the actual work on your project. With regard to fees, it is important to know that most architects base their fees on a percentage of the total cost of construction. Therefore, you need to know that architects often have little incentive to cut costs because to do so only cuts their fee. This is why the owner needs to be well represented in the process.

In addition, you need to understand that your architect will use a number of engineering specialties on your project. These will include MEP engineers (who will design the mechanical systems, the electrical systems, and the plumbing systems in the building), structural engineers who will design the supporting structures of the building, the civil engineers who will deal with items such as site plans, paving, building elevations, utility lines and the like, landscape architects to design landscaped areas, acoustical consultants to help with building acoustics and sound and, in some cases, traffic engineers. At some architectural firms, these consultants may be on staff, in most cases the architects hire outside consultants. In either scenario, how these people are paid is an important contract issue. It is typically best to pay the architect one all-in fee and have the architect hire and pay the consultants. In this way, the architect is responsible for managing the consultants (it is the architect's fault if the consultant does not perform) and is accountable for the consultant's mistakes (the architect is on the hook if the MEP engineer makes a mistake).

After you have selected a core team and you have a good idea of what you want to build, it is time to get started. The first step is to find a site for your project.

2. The Site Selection Process

Together with your construction team, you will be able to determine what type of building you need. In turn, that will tell you how much land you need to acquire. Your architect will be able to estimate a needed land area. Once you know how much land you need, you can begin a search for property. I strongly recommend that a highly qualified real estate brokerage firm be retained for this process. It is important that the firm specialize in commercial real estate deals and not be a residential broker. There is simply a world of difference between dealing in large commercial land tracts and selling houses. The bottom line is that you need someone who knows the market and the players and can help you get the right deal, not just any deal.

When going through the search process it is important to look at a number of sites and not to get "married" to a particular site. A savvy seller who senses that you are unwilling to walk away can often extract a high price. Also, you need to consider issues such as access to the site (can you get your congregation on and off of the site) and both the availability and capability of utilities. For example, it can easily add hundreds of thousands of dollars to a project if the church is required to extend or expand utilities in order to adequately serve a site. Generally, the city has no obligation to pay to bring utilities to your site.

It is also very important to consider the long-term potential of a site. You need to consider the possibility of future needs of the church in deciding if the site is large enough. Recently, more savvy churches have also wisely considered the investment/resell potential of a site. Very often the purchase of a very large site that is a little off of the beaten path today can prove to be a much better long-term deal that a smaller tract in a prime location. Using this strategy, some churches have benefited by selling part of their excess property as development approached their previously remote location.

3.The Purchase Contract

After the site has been selected and a price agreed to, you need a skilled real estate lawyer to negotiate the contract terms. The purchase contract for a tract of raw land will include most of the same matters that are addressed in a purchase contract to buy a building. For this reason, the details will not be rehashed at this point. However, a couple of additional points need to be made. First, the contract should clarify what you are and are not getting. This can include issues such as development or water rights and whether the property comes with certain encumbrances such as easements or development responsibilities. In addition, the contract should specify whether utilities are present on the site and, if not, who is responsible for extending the utilities. Next, if a zoning change is required, the contract should specify who is required to obtain the change (this can be a significant expense item).

Due Diligence

As with the purchase of an existing building, a due diligence review needs to be conducted under your lawyer's guidance. This will include all of the steps previously mentioned with regard to purchasing an existing property. In addition to the steps listed under the purchase of an existing property, the following additional steps need to be taken:

a.Soil testing needs to be conducted. This is critical because the type of soil present can vary the cost of construction by millions of dollars. For example, highly elastic clay soils often require extensive foundation work that can result in significant budget increases. Depending upon whether such challenging soil conditions are common to your area, you may want to consider an alternate site that does not require you to spend extra funds on your foundation. At a minimum, you want to take such conditions into account when negotiating or re-negotiating your deal. When you find such conditions during your due diligence investigation, do not hesitate to go back to the bargaining table with the seller. If the soil condition was reflected in the initial agreed upon price, it should have been disclosed up-front. If it was not disclosed, there is no reason not to go back and re-work the deal.

b.In most cases, raw land that has never been occupied is unlikely to have an environmental problem. However, it is possible that a hazardous use, such as an old gas station, was located on the property at one time and has since been removed. In addition, some farming and drilling operations can leave behind hazardous waste. For these reasons, you should not overlook the step of obtaining a Phase One Environmental Site Assessment on the property. Always keep in mind that the officers and board members of a church can be held personally liable for the cost of an environmental cleanup. However, by obtaining an environmental site assessment that indicates that no evidence exists of contamination, the church (and its officers and directors) can avail themselves of a "safe harbor" under the environmental laws as an innocent landowner.

c.The single biggest disaster that you can encounter in the building process is not being able to build on property that you just paid good money to buy. Accordingly, the most important due diligence step in dealing with raw land is obtaining the needed governmental approvals to build your planned facility. Ideally, you want to have all necessary approvals, most importantly a building permit, in hand before you close on the property. In this way, you insure that you can, in fact, build what you want.

Do not let sellers or brokers bluff you on this point. All too often seller will claim that, of course, you can build a church on this property. They will also try to get you to remove the contingency from the contract that says that you do not have to close until you get a permit. Understand two important points. First, there are no certainties when it comes to obtaining approvals from city government officials. Government officials are people and people do strange and unexplainable things from time to time. Moreover churches do not benefit cities. Churches cost cities money. Churches remove valuable property from the tax rolls while still requiring the city to provide costly services such as fire, police, streets etc. The result is that some city officials may not be inclined to bend over backwards to help you.

Second, every sophisticated user of real estate always waits until they have a permit in hand before they close. The reason is simple, whether they are shopping center developers, restaurant operators, or retail stores, they do not want land they cannot use as they intend. Therefore, virtually every contract with a sophisticated user (someone who is going to use the land as opposed to a speculator) contains a contingency that allows the buyer to back out of the deal if the necessary government approvals cannot be obtained.

As soon as the land is under contract, you and your team need to start the process of working with the local government to obtain approvals for your planned project. You will need to verify that the zoning allows for construction of the type of building that you are planning. You will need to be especially mindful of building height restrictions, parking requirements, sign restrictions, landscape requirements and restrictions on the use of certain building materials.

Any large growing church will have on-going dealings with its local city government. Therefore, it is critical that you begin to develop good working relationships with both staff level city workers and elected officials. To be successful, you will need to work both ends of city government. Both staff and elected officials have power and can make your life pleasant or difficult.

Like everything else in life, you need to deal with city officials in a balanced manner. Do not allow them to push you around, because some will try. Likewise, you need to choose your battles carefully. You do not want to harm a valuable relationship over an insignificant matter. Sometimes you may have to fight, but if you do, make sure there are spoils to be won.

For the most part, however, I urge you to spend the time to develop relationships. Relationships will be your greatest ally if you have a problem. This means getting to know each and every city council member in your town. It means getting to know top city staff members. This process can be aided greatly by finding the right lawyer to help you obtain city approvals. In every city in every state, there are one or two lawyers who conduct a lot of land use business with that city. Ask your regular attorney to help you find the best land use attorney around. You can also attend a few city council meetings and see who is representing a lot of developers who are working on big projects. Remember, you are not looking for a fighter or impressive speaker. You are looking for the lawyer who works his relationships.

The bottom-line is to make sure that you are straight with the city before you buy. If you have already bought the property, take the same steps. However, you may have to live with some things that you don't like. Again, relationships will often save you.

GET YOUR FINANCING

As soon as the contract is signed (or preferably before), you need to be pursuing your financing. If you have followed the steps above, you have already had conversations with your banker and you know that the deal that you want to do is at least feasible. You know that your church can afford the purchase and can afford its debt service obligations.

At this time, you have two basic alternatives when seeking financing for your church facility. The most common alternative is traditional bank financing. This involves exactly what it sounds like, going to your local bank (hopefully you have some relationship with your banker) and seeking a loan. The alternative is to seek church bond financing. Under this scenario, you employ a bond underwriter to issue bonds that are sold to the public to fund your purchase/project.

Historically, banks did not actively seek church loans and bonds were the most common financing mechanism for churches. However, over the last few years banks have become much more active in church financing and, as a result, only a handful of viable companies still exist in the church bond financing business. The reason for the demise of the church bond business is the expense of bond financing (bond companies typically charge 5-7% of the loan proceeds as up-front fees as opposed to Ω-1% of the proceeds for bank financing) and the fact that banks now are charging competitive interest rates to churches in an effort to compete in the marketplace. In the past, a bond program could turn out cheaper for a church (despite the high up-front fees) because the banks did not want the church business and, as a result, charged higher interest rates.

As long as the large commercial banks remain active in the church loan business, it will be difficult for the bond companies to compete and this area will continue to be dominated by the banks. That being the case, a lengthy discussion of bond financing is unnecessary. It is enough to say that bond financing probably only makes sense if you are having trouble obtaining bank financing.

Depending on the size of the loan, the bank will typically require the following items in order to begin processing your loan application:

A copy of your church organizational documents, that is your articles of incorporation and bylaws.

Financial statements for the church for the past three years (audited financial statements are greatly preferred). Banks place far greater faith in churches who have their financial statements audited on an annual basis by a respected CPA firm. For large loans, banks will typically require audited financial statements to be delivered to them on an annual basis until the loan is paid-off. The reason is simple, the bank wants to know that your organization is financially sound and an audit is one way to do that.

A copy of your purchase contract for the land or building.

The bank will typically order an appraisal of the property to verify value. Please remember that a bank can only rely on an appraisal that it ordered. Therefore, do not waste money by getting your own appraisal if you plan to use bank financing.

The bank will also want your Phase One Site Assessment to meet its criteria. Therefore, consult with your bank before ordering the site assessment to make sure that you use an approved firm.

Banks typically order background checks on the pastor and key employees.

Once the bank has your church's financial statements and they know what the deal is, the loan officer will prepare an internal loan package and seek approval. Banks vary in their approval process. Most banks use a committee approach where a majority of a committee has to approve any loan. Other banks use individual approval where certain officers in the bank have the right to approve any loan up to a certain dollar amount. For example, one officer may have approval up to $1,000,000, but a higher officer may be needed to approve any loan up to $5,000,000 and yet a higher officer is required to go above that amount.

Once the bank has approved your loan request, the bank will issue a Loan Commitment Letter. In that letter, the bank will agree to make the loan, on the terms stated in the letter, as long as certain conditions are met. The terms of the letter are very important.

The letter tells you what the terms of the loan are. It is important to remember that the terms of the bank's commitment letter are negotiable. If you do not like something in the commitment, negotiate with the bank to get it changed.

Do not limit yourself to one bank. Because most people really want the loan, they forget that the bank is in the business of making loans, it is how banks make money. Instead of chips or autoparts, banks sell loans to individuals and companies. Therefore you need to remember that banking is like every other business in the business world, you need competition to get the best deal. When the bank knows that they are the only player for your loan, the bank will take advantage of the lack of competition.

The key points on a loan that can be negotiated are the interest rate, the amortization schedule, the loan term (or length of the loan), whether the loan is fixed or floating, and the loan covenants. Most people are familiar with the first term, the interest rate. This is the amount of interest, on an annual basis, that the bank is charging for the use if its money. As interest rates change daily, it would be worthless to try and make statements here concerning what is or is not a good interest rate. However, the key point to remember is that an established church, with good credit and more than ample cash flow should be charged an interest rate that is close to the bank's prime rate. If you are being charged a rate well above prime (more than 1-2 points above prime), either the bank views your loan as risky or may be overcharging you in the belief that you have no alternatives. It should be noted that rates will be slightly higher for smaller loans (under $1-2 million).

The amortization schedule is the time period for repayment that is used to calculate the actual payments. It is common for the actual loan to have a shorter time period. For instance, most banks are short-term lenders, that is they do not make 20 or 30 year loans. Instead, a bank will make a five year loan (the loan must be paid-off or refinanced within 5 years) with a 25 year amortization. In that case, the payments are based on an amortization of 25 years (the payments are calculated as if the loan was for 25 years) but the loan is due in 5 years. Banks are not in the business of taking long-term risks, therefore they want to be able to re-evaluate the loan after 5 years.

The decision of whether to go with a floating or fixed rate loan is one of calculating risk. Floating rate loans always have lower initial interest rates than fixed rate loans. With a floating rate loan, you take the interest rate risk. That is, if interest rates go up, so does your interest rate and, consequently, your loan payment. On the other hand, with a fixed rate loan, the bank takes the interest rate risk. No matter what happens to market rates, you always pay the same rate. The cost is a higher initial interest rate. I suggest that you have a discussion with your banker and accountant to weigh the relative risks and rewards of each option.

In some cases, you may be able to choose a blended approach by dividing your loan into two parts — one fixed and one floating. In addition, your banker or investment advisor may be able to help you hedge the risk of a floating rate loan by making investments that would earn you money if interest moved in a direction that would cost you money under your loan.

Loan covenants are restrictions that the bank will place upon your organization. For example, most large loans include debt covenants that limit the amount of additional debt that you can take on without the bank's written approval. Banks ask for such provisions because they do not want you to get too far in debt and, as a result, be unable to pay what you owe on your loan. For the same reason, the bank may place a limit on the amount of money that you can spend on capital items (major long-term purchases) without the bank's consent.

After you have negotiated the loan terms, you should receive a Loan Commitment from your bank. Do not rely on a verbal commitment or on a letter of interest. You want a letter that says that the bank has agreed to make the loan if certain things happen — typically title matters, no change in financial condition, your putting up the down payment and so forth.

Once you have a loan commitment, have completed your due diligence, have obtained the necessary approvals, you are ready to close the deal. The closing will follow the same steps listed above for the purchase of an existing property.

GIFTS OF REAL ESTATE

One common real estate issue for churches is the gift to the church of real estate. When someone wants to make a gift a real property to the church, follow these steps:

Complete your due diligence just as if you were buying the property. Specifically, you need to know if the property has liens against it (that the church would have to pay), if the property taxes are current and what the amount of the taxes are on an annual basis (it is unlikely you can exempt such property and the church will be responsible for paying taxes going forward), and if the property has environmental problems (more than one loving donor has attempted to "give" their problem to their church).

Have a real estate broker give you an estimate of the market value of the property and the likely time period that will be required to sell the property. If the property is not marketable, you are just getting the right to pay property taxes.

Inform the donor that he or she is responsible for obtaining a fair market value appraisal of the property for tax deduction. The church cannot pay for the appraisal. It must be obtained by and paid for by the donor.

CHAPTER FOUR

Minimizing Your Risk of Liability

David O. Middlebrook

The Bad News

The bad news is simple. Churches are no longer immune to the legal wrangling that takes place in all other aspects of secular society. The myth that religious institutions are somehow protected from our "sue happy" society will not protect you in a lawsuit. The statistics are clear: in a world of mega-churches, multi-million dollar ministries and outrageous monetary judgments, people are more willing than ever before to file suit against you. And why shouldn't they? It usually only takes about $150 to file a lawsuit in your local courthouse, and if the plaintiff wins, many times he won't even have to pay attorneys' fees.

The Good News

There is no need to take cover and hide — waiting in fear for the first assault! To the contrary: You can minister in confidence if you have put in place policies and procedures to protect you legally, policies that will become your best ally if you follow them. While at first the task may seem daunting, churches and ministries are not defenseless. God has called His people to excellence, and this calling includes the framework of your ministry. In protecting your church against the threat of a lawsuit, you are also creating an atmosphere of professionalism which in turn, will attract higher quality employees and inspire a stronger work ethic. As such, with education and initiative, you will not only protect against a lawsuit, you will equip yourself to run a more efficient organization. Everyone wins.

Proverbs 3:21-26 makes this promise, "My child, don't lose sight of good planning and insight. Hang on to them, for they fill your life and bring you honor and respect. They keep you safe on your way and keep your feet from stumbling. You can lie down without fear and enjoy pleasant dreams. You need not be afraid of disaster or the destruction that comes upon the wicked for the LORD is your security. He will keep your foot from being caught in a trap." Your preparation will be honored.

With this promise in hand, let's enter into a discussion of the major legal areas with potential to affect your church or ministry.

The Church as an employer — your duties under Federal Law

It can be argued that no area of the law has undergone more expansion in recent years than the laws regulating private employers in their relationship to their employees. Churches should recognize that not only has Congress acted on this subject, but state legislatures and local governments have also enacted laws affecting the employment relationship. A church's failure to take into consideration such laws and regulations exposes itself to a significant risk of liability as it relates to employment decisions.

1.State Laws — An employer's right to fire an employee is subject to certain limits under statutory and case law. Many states have imposed various limitations on an employer's right to discharge an employee. Examples of these limitations include: (a) workers' compensation; (b) state military service; (c) court appearances or jury service; (d) union membership or non-membership.

2.Federal laws—Do they apply to your church

A.Title VII of the 1964 Civil Rights Act

1.What is it and does it apply to your church? The statute states: "It shall be an unlawful employment practice for an employer to fail or refuse to hire or to discharge any individual, or otherwise to discriminate against any individual with respect to his compensation, terms, conditions, or privileges of employment, because of such individuals race, color, religion, sex, or national origin."

2.Fifteen (15) employee requirement. - A church must have fifteen (15) or more full or part time employees for each working day in each of twenty (20) or more calendar weeks in the current or proceeding calendar year. But note that under the ruling in Walters v. Metropolitan Educational Enterprises, Inc., 519 U.S. 202 (Jan. 14, 1997), all employees on a weekly payroll should be counted in determining whether an entity can be sued under Title VII, regardless of how many days employees actually work or get paid in a given week.

3."Affecting commerce" requirement -This requirement is subject to determination by the court. In some cases, merely utilizing the services of out of state vendors, or engaging in telephonic interstate conversations, theoretically, could result in a decision by a judge that the church is involved in affecting commerce.

As such, any church that employs fifteen or more full or part time employees should consider itself covered by Title VII. Further, as a "safe harbor" approach, all churches should consider complying with Title VII rather than subjecting themselves to a lawsuit that would require them to prove that they are not within its jurisdictional requirements. 4.Equal Employment Opportunity Commission - The Equal Employment Opportunity Commission enforces Title VII. If your church or ministry is notified that a complaint has been filed with the Equal Employment Opportunity Commission, it is recommended that legal counsel be immediately consulted to assist in the investigation and response procedure. Under no circumstances should the charge be ignored or the allegation minimized.

5.Permissible Religious Discrimination - Title VII, Section 702 of the Civil Rights Act specifically exempts religious corporations, associations, educational institutions or societies with respect to the employment of individuals. Therefore, a church may discriminate on the basis of religion in all employment decisions.

B.Age Discrimination (ADEA) - Congress enacted the "Age Discrimination In Employment Act" (ADEA) in 1967. It applies to employers with twenty (20) or more employees in an industry affecting commerce. The ADEA prohibits employers from discriminating on the basis of age against employees or employee applicants who are over forty (40) years of age regarding hiring, firing, compensation, or terms, conditions or privileges of employment. As a general rule there is no upper limit on age. Therefore, it is a violation of the ADEA, except under very narrow circumstances, for an employer to force an employee into retirement, even if that employee is qualified under a pension or retirement benefit plan.

Further, it is a violation for an employer to fail to provide the same insurance and retirement benefits for all employees of all ages. Any church or ministry considering a reduction in force ("RIF") must also consider the implications of such a RIF on employees covered by the ADEA or the Older Worker Benefit Protection Act of 1990. It is strongly recommended that any consideration of performing a RIF be made only with the assistance of competent legal counsel.

C.Americans With Disabilities Act (ADA) - The ADA provides that no employer that has fifteen (15) or more employees may discriminate against any "qualified individual with a disability" in regard to "job application procedures, the hiring, the advancement, or discharge of employees, employee compensation, job training and other terms, conditions, and privileges of employment." The term "disability" is defined by the Act as a "physical or mental impairment that substantially limits one or more of the major life activities of such individual."

If a qualified applicant is disabled, the law requires an employer to make "reasonable accommodations" to employ the disabled applicant unless those accommodations would impose an "undue hardship" on the employer.

The ADA also prohibits discrimination in public accommodations. However, churches are specifically exempted from this provision. Church administrators should be familiar with state or local laws regarding this issue.

Acquired Immune Deficiency Syndrome (AIDS) - Churches that are covered by the Americans with Disabilities Act may not discriminate against an individual because he or she has AIDS or because that person has a family member with the disease. Additionally, most states and some local ordinances prohibit discrimination against persons with AIDS.

Fair Labor And Standards Act (FLSA) - The Fair Labor And Standards Act (FLSA), most generally referred to as "wage and hour laws," is a very large and complex area of the law. Additionally, most states have enacted their own wage and hour laws of which churches should be very familiar. Churches should work closely with legal counsel and their CPA to determine categories of "exempt" and "non-exempt" employees and to conform compliance to various provisions of the wage and hour laws promulgated by the FLSA. Churches that operate day care centers or church schools should be especially concerned about compliance with FLSA requirements.

F. Family Medical & Leave Act (FMLA) - This legislation enacted and effective as of August 1993, requires employers with fifty (50) or more employees to provide up to twelve (12) weeks of unpaid leave to eligible employees because of the birth or adoption of a child or because of a serious health condition of the employee or the employee's child, parent or spouse.

"Eligible employees" covered by the Act must have been employed at least twelve (12) months by the covered employer and have worked at least 1250 hours during the previous 12-month period.

Note: The Act does not require covered employers to provide paid leave for employees qualified under the Act. However, violations of the law can result in damages for lost wages, salary benefits, compensation, court costs and attorneys fees.

Churches or ministries with fifty (50) employees or more should work closely with legal counsel to assure compliance with the technical requirements of the law and to avoid violation of its mandates.

G.Immigration Law (IRCA) - The Immigration Reform And Control Act was enacted in 1986 and all churches and religious organizations are subject to the rules contained within the Act. The IRCA applies to all employers employing one or more persons. Therefore, all churches are required to comply with the statute's regulations.

The law requires employers, including churches, to do five things:

1.Complete the top half of Form I-9 on or before the date the employee starts work.

2.Check original documents establishing every new employee's identity and eligibility to work.

3.Complete the bottom half of Form I-9 by certifying that you inspected the original documents verifying the employee's identity and eligibility to work.

4.Retain every Form I-9 for at least three years.

5.Present a Form I-9 for inspection to an Immigration and Naturalization Service or Department of Labor officer upon request. (NOTE: I-9 is not filed with the government. The burden is placed upon the employer to retain the document for inspection by the appropriate government employee).

All employees, whether U.S. citizens or not, are required to complete an I-9 Form and provide the required documents. Self employed or contractual workers are not required to complete an I-9 Form. The I-9 Form need only be completed by people you actually hire and not by job applicants. Failure to comply with the law will result in monetary penalties. Employers which knowingly hire illegal aliens face fines up to $10,000 for each illegal alien hired. The proceeding is an overview of the law, and if you have specific questions please consult with a qualified attorney who is familiar with the complete requirements of IRCA and the churches obligations under it.

H.Pregnancy Discrimination Act (PDA) - In 1978, Congress enacted the "Pregnancy Discrimination Act" which amended Title VII and broadened sex discrimination to include discrimination on the basis of pregnancy, childbirth related medical conditions. This Act does not require paid or unpaid maternity leave, but does require that pregnancy be treated the same as any other medical condition. If your church or ministry has more than fifty (50) employees, then the "Family Medical and Leave Act" is implicated and you may have additional obligations to pregnant employees.

*One Very Important Tip

PASTOR - CHURCH EXCEPTION

The First Amendment guarantee of religious freedom is so powerful that the courts of this country are hesitant to interfere in a church's decision regarding the employment of a minister. Consequently, the Federal employment laws previously discussed, provide very little, if any, protection to pastors from unfair or discriminatory employment practices by churches.

Absent an employment agreement, churches are free to consider a pastor's sex, age, race, etc. in making employment decisions. The reasoning for this exception is based on the rationale that to permit pastors to bring suit against the church and bring into question the church's employment decisions would give rise to serious constitutional questions, thus leading to entanglement between the church and the State which is forbidden by the First Amendment. Therefore, it is crucial for pastors to maintain updated employment agreements with their churches.

PRE-EMPLOYMENT PROTECTIONS

The following is a list of several pre-employment protections the church employer should use not only to protect the church from later litigation, but also to ensure that quality employees are hired from the beginning of the process.

1.Legal Employment Applications - The application's purpose is to elicit job-related information from an applicant to enable the employer to make an informed hiring decision. Applications affect how much information an employer can collect regarding an applicant's personal life and experiences.

There are many constraints placed on employer inquiries involving such topics as age, marital status, pregnancy, disability, and others by federal and state laws. The church should be very careful about its pre-employment inquiries, and have an attorney review its current application.

To preserve at-will employment relations, the application should prominently contain at-will employment disclaimer language. This disclaims that the application is an employment contract of any kind.

Please note that it is not a good idea to keep applications "on file." This is usually a poor practice and is often not, in fact, utilized by most employers. Additionally, representing to a candidate that you are going to keep his or her application "on file" may lead to a charge of discrimination if it can be established that the church employer did not actually review previous applications that were kept "on file" when a new position became open. It is my belief that this is a poor practice and should be eliminated.

2.Who to Interview - It is not necessary to have a face-to-face interview with every applicant who completes a job application. If an applicant does not meet the minimum job application requirements, it is not necessary to meet with them. As such, it is a good practice to develop a detailed set of minimum job requirements for each position that you are interviewing to fill. In this way, the church can screen applicants over the telephone and determine whether or not they meet the stated minimum job applications for the position which is being offered. Candidates who meet the minimum job applications can be invited to set an appointment and be interviewed. Candidates who do not meet the minimum job application should be told so over the phone and thanked for their inquiry.

In the same way, if the church receives an application for employment through the mail with a resume, the church should attempt to determine whether or not the candidate meets the specified minimum job application requirements. If so, an appointment should be scheduled. If not, the applicant should be called and informed that they are not going to be considered for the position because they do not qualify.

3.Establish Written Interview Protocol - As a general rule, the interviewer for the church should focus on questions which identify the applicant's ability to perform the tasks related to the job in question. In this connection, the job description should be utilized as a checklist to determine whether the applicant possesses the appropriate skills and experience for the position. Additionally, a standard protocol should be developed for every interview conducted by the church. The interviewer should not ask any questions which are not job related. Interview notes should be taken to help the interviewer to differentiate between candidates and to document the reasoning and rationale for selection decisions should a charge of discrimination be brought against the church. Note taking should be limited, however, to job specific issues. A memorandum should be prepared following each interview that summarizes the information that was elicited during the interview. This memorandum, along with interview notes, and the application should be retained in the event that a complaint is filed by the applicant claiming discrimination.

Federal law regulates the type of questions considered permissible during an employment interview. Prohibited lines of inquiry include questions regarding age, race, sex, disability and national origin. A church is permitted to inquire as to whether or not the applicant is a Christian.

4.References - Reference checks of applicants by the church represent another effort to compile and verify the most complete and accurate information regarding the applicant. Requesting detailed references from former employers is one precaution a church employer can take during the hiring process to limit its vulnerability to employment litigation. By failing to request references, the church may risk negligent hiring liability. References should be checked before the church makes a final job offer.

This area of the law, although a routine matter for most church employers, is filled with legal pitfalls. Most employers have adopted what is referred to as a "neutral reference policy" and will only release information related to the dates of employment, position and salary of the employee at the time of separation. Employers have adopted such policies to avoid lawsuits for defamation (libel and slander) related to an employee's work performance. It is often possible to overcome such neutral reference policies by obtaining a release from job applicants at the time they complete the job application that permits former employers, when contacted, to disclose information and opinions as they relate to the applicant's job performance. At the time of hire, a new employee should be required to complete a form that authorizes the church to release employment data to prospective employers.

5.Policy for Rejection of Candidates - Each candidate that was not selected for the particular job in question should receive a letter in the mail rejecting his application. It is not necessary and not advisable that the rejected candidate be informed of the reasoning for the rejection of their application. Rather, merely thank them for the courtesy of applying for the position.

6.Drug Testing - It has been estimated that between 60 and 80 percent of the United States population is using a psychoactive substance either at work or at home. To select the best method for controlling drugs and alcohol at work, a church employer must ascertain the risks and the attendant costs. Some common risks of drugs or alcohol on the job are: (1) workers' compensation claims for injuries, (2) customer complaints or injuries, (3) physical damage, (4) theft, and (5) poor job performance. Some new risks are: (1) liability for accidents caused by an intoxicated employee sent home, (2) punitive damages for entrusting a company vehicle to an employee who has a DWI conviction but has never had a drink at work, (3) workers' compensation claims for addiction, (4) unemployment claims, (5) violations of ERISA, and (6) violations of OSHA.

Points to cover in every church drug testing policy:

Prohibition of the use of drugs or alcohol

Prohibition of possession of drugs and related paraphernalia

Prohibition of sale of drugs or alcohol

Fitness for duty

When to test

Types of tests

Who can require a test

Chain of custody of test results

Re-testing

Who will do the testing

Confidentiality

Criminal prosecution

Over-the-counter or prescribed medication

Searches

Compliance with applicable law

Consent and release forms

Offer Letters - If your church sends formal offer letters to applicants you want to hire, you should be aware of the following things:

The letter should contain no promises or guarantees

The letter should contain at-will employment language

The letter should contain language that the stated salary is "computational"

The letter should state that the position is "subject to change at the discretion of employer."

If an offer letter contains promises of employment and salary without some limiting language as suggested above, the letter may be used to enforce an employment contract against the church.

PROTECTIONS DURING EMPLOYMENT

1.Probationary Period

All newly hired employees should be classified as "introductory" employees. This means that their performance is being scrutinized for some introductory period — usually 90 days — to determine whether or not continued employment is warranted.

Note: this does not mean you can violate state and federal law because the employee is on probation.

In addition to receiving their agreed on compensation, the "introductory" employee receives all legally mandated benefits such as workers' compensation, social security, Medicare benefits, etc. The introductory employee does not receive, however, other church benefits unless and until they satisfactorily complete their period of probation.

2.Performance Reviews & Employee Files

A.Performance Reviews - At a minimum, a performance appraisal should occur at least once a year. Although performance reviews and appraisals appear to be time consuming, they are an excellent way to control the salary structure of a church by defining minimum performance goals. Also, they are useful tools in a well-established progressive discipline program and when properly documented, can be used to convince an employee that protesting a dismissal would be futile.

Employee Files - The church must keep accurate and complete employee files. These files should be kept in a secure area and should include the employee's original application, copies of the employee's annual performance reviews, all memorandums relating to disciplinary actions taken toward the employee, complete insurance application forms, copies of the employees I-9 forms, etc. Federal law does not require employees be given access to their employee files, however, some states do require such access. If your church is in one of those states, then we recommend each employee be given two employee files, an "A" file containing general employment documentation and a "B" file which contains management information, including sensitive employee information.

3.Progressive Discipline

The starting point when considering the implementation of a progressive discipline plan is securing proper documentation. Written performance appraisals, memos to the employees, records of absence or tardiness, etc., are all critical in providing proper supporting documentation of unsatisfactory employee job performance.

When disciplining employees, focus on behavior and not personality or attitudes. Prior to termination, it is recommended that each employee receive the following:

Oral warning: include the specifics of their inadequate performance as well as a time deadline to improve their performance. The oral warning should be documented by way of memorandum to the employee's file.

Written warning: if the oral warning fails to remedy the employee's performance problems, then a written warning should be prepared which references the date of the oral warning as well as the information communicated to the employee at the time of the oral warning. The written warning should contain an outline of inadequate performance as well as a time deadline for the employee to remedy his performance as well as the consequences that will result from his or her failure to remedy performance. The written warning should be signed by the employee and should be delivered with a witness present. If the employee refuses to sign the written warning, the witness can be utilized to provide a statement documenting same.

Probation/suspension without pay: if, after giving an oral warning and a written warning, the church may elect to put a particular employee on probation or suspension without pay in lieu of terminating the employee from his or her position. Again, the decision to place an employee on probation or suspension without pay should be communicated by written memorandum signed by the employee. The probation notice should be delivered in the presence of a witness and in the same way, if the employee refuses to sign the memorandum, the witness should document same memorandum to the employee's file.

4.Discharge

After completing the 3-step disciplinary process described above, it may become necessary to discharge an employee. On the other hand, some conduct by an employee may be so egregious so as to warrant immediate termination without notice. Regardless of which situation exists, once the decision is made to terminate an employee, the church must proceed carefully to avoid or reduce the risk of litigation as a result of effectuating the termination decision.

Protections at Time of Termination

1.Pre-termination Investigation

Investigate and substantiate the facts.

2.Exit Interview

An exit interview should be conducted and the conversation with the employee should be fully documented.

Sometimes, churches are forced to undergo reductions in force (RIF). Although less emotional for an employee, it still results in the employee losing his or her position. It is important for employers who are under Title VII to consult an attorney to promote fairness in the decision making process and to avoid or minimize the likelihood of claims or charges of discrimination in the selection process of employees to be included in the RIF.

3.Termination Reports

Document reason and give details including final incident, dates, times, and witnesses. Indicate dates of warnings and by whom.

4.Severance Agreements

Often, an employee will request to resign rather than be terminated. Depending on the circumstances, it may be in the church's best interest to permit the employee to resign. If so, the church should secure a written document from the employee stating that he or she has elected to resign his or her position. It is recommended that this instrument be prepared by legal counsel.

Additionally, although not legally obligated to do so by Federal or State law, a church may elect to pay severance pay to an employee at the time of separation. Generally, the purpose of this is to secure a release from the employee of any and all claims that he or she may have related to their tenure at the church. Again, this instrument should only be prepared after consultation with qualified legal counsel to avoid violation of federal laws such as the Older Worker's Benefit Protection Act (OWBPA).COMPENSATION

In recent years, the IRS has been expressing concern about the manner in which non-profit organizations govern themselves and how it affects the revenue of the federal government. The following concerns have been identified by the IRS:

Excessive compensation issues. The IRS is clearly concerned about the payment of excessive compensation by exempt organizations. Salary is only one component that the IRS will consider when determining if compensation is excessive. They will consider all payments of any kind and for any reason that direct the resources of the organization toward an individual. That means that every benefit received is thrown in the pot for compensation purposes.

Fringe benefits. The IRS has expressed concern over the failure by many exempt organizations to recognize that some fringe benefits constitute taxable income to their officers. These include private use of a vehicle that is owned or leased by the charity, payment of an individual's automobile insurance premiums, and a charity's payment of an officer's personal expenses, including some household expenses, country club dues, maid services, and vacations.

Failure to file Form 990. The penalty for failure to file the Form 990 has been increased to $100 per day with a maximum fine of $50,000 per year.

In 1996 new legislation was enacted entitled the "Tax-Payer's Bill of Rights 2." As part of this new law, for the very first time, the IRS imposed "intermediate sanctions" against individuals involved in certain types of transactions with churches and other tax-exempt organizations. Essentially, these "intermediate sanctions" take the form of excise taxes that may be imposed in lieu of, or in addition to, revocation of the organization's tax exempt status.

Intermediate Sanctions. Essentially, the legislation imposes a series of excise taxes, also referred to as "intermediate sanctions," on individuals who are involved in any transaction that results in any "disqualified person" receiving an "excess benefit" from a non-profit organization. For purposes of this new tax law, a "disqualified person" receives an "excess benefit" if that person, directly or indirectly receives an economic benefit from a non-profit organization that exceeds the value of the consideration received by the non-profit.

For example, if a church pays its pastor $200,000 per year (being the sum of the pastor's total compensation package including salary, housing allowance, benefits, fringe benefits, etc.) and the value of the pastor's service is determined by the IRS to only be $100,000, the pastor has received an "excess benefit" of $100,000.

One of the problems with this law is the severity of the penalties involved. For each "excess benefit" transaction, the following series of draconian penalty taxes are involved:

1.The "disqualified person" who receives the excess benefit must repay the benefit to the organization, and, in addition, pay an excise tax to the IRS equal to 25% of the excess benefit.

2.The "organization managers" who participated in and were aware of the excess benefit transaction are liable for an excise tax equal to 10% of the excess benefit, up to a maximum of $10,000.00 for each excess benefit transaction.

If the "disqualified person" who received the excess benefit does not repay the organization within the same tax period (defined as the date of the transaction to the date of assessment or notice of deficiency), the IRS imposes a 200% excise tax on the excess benefit received by the disqualified person.

If the organization pays or reimburses an employee for the payment of the excess benefit penalty taxes, the payment or reimbursement is itself considered an excess benefit unless it is included in the employee's taxable compensation the year the payment or reimbursement is made. The employee's total compensation will still be subject to the "reasonable compensation" requirement.

To better illustrate the potential impact of this law, recall the example above of the pastor whose total compensation is $200,000, but the reasonable value of his service to the church is only $100,000. Under this new law, the pastor must repay the $100,000 excess benefit to his church and a $25,000 excise tax to the IRS. If the pastor does not or cannot repay the excess benefit to his church within the same tax period, then a $200,000.00 tax is imposed by the IRS.

Mr. Marcus Owen, director of the IRS Exempt Organizations Division in Washington, D.C., at a recent conference stated that the service intends to "shock the conscience" of individuals in non-profits who receive excessive salaries, perks, and benefits.

STEPS YOUR CHURCH SHOULD TAKE TO MINIMIZE THE RISK OF SEXUAL HARASSMENT CHARGES

Most employers are well aware of the public's elevated awareness of to sexual harassment in the workplace as evidenced by the ever-rising number of claims filed against employers. Contrary to expectations, our experience reveals that churches, as employers, generally do not enjoy a workplace less prone to these claims, though most churches assume that their adherence to biblical doctrines would preclude harassing behavior.

Your church, especially if it has never faced a sexual harassment claim, should be aware of important developments in the law that, if utilized, provide your church with a measure of protection in the unfortunate event a claim is leveled by one of your employees.

Specifically, the holdings of recent U.S. Supreme Court cases have set forth an affirmative defense for employers in defending a sexual harassment claim. However, to take full advantage of the newly recognized defenses, you must take certain preventative steps before, not after, your church is named in an accusation of harassment.

The affirmative defense insulates employers from liability or damages in cases where sexual harassment occurred but no tangible negative employment action was taken against the employee, such as discharge, demotion, or reassignment. To claim protection, the employer must show three things:

That prior to the claim, the employer had taken reasonable care to prevent harassing behavior

That the employer, once aware of any inappropriate interaction, acted promptly to correct such behavior

And that the employee unreasonably failed to take advantage of any preventative or corrective opportunities provided by the employer.

Clearly, the potential benefit your church could receive from this affirmative defense turns on the degree to which you have established an anti-harassment policy before the claim arises. When implementing your policy, we recommend adopting a "zero tolerance" plan with at least each of these features:

1. Easy to comprehend illustrations of harassing behavior

2. The church's policy statement against all such conduct

3. A reporting procedure that allows the employee to bypass a harassing supervisor

4. A procedure for the anti-harassment policy to be explained and distributed to all employees

5. Training for managers to recognize and report wrongful conduct

6. Mandatory monitoring of supervisors by top management

7. A plan for prompt corrective action in the event of an allegation.

One important, but often overlooked issue, is maintaining an updated sexual harassment policy. If your office does not monitor the current EEOC guidelines, and implement their definitions and suggestions into the policy, a court could find that the policy is neither reasonably designed nor reasonably effectual. As such, the church could find itself liable in a lawsuit because it was not taking "reasonable steps" to prevent harassment in its offices.

An example of the importance of maintaining an updated harassment policy occurred in 2000, when the U.S. Court of Appeals found that a company's policy was an insufficient means of preventing sexual harassment because it did not address recently published EEOC guidelines. The harassed employee, Ms. Smith, was subjected to a barrage of threats and gender-based insults while under the supervision of Mr. Scoggins, the defendant. Mr. Scoggins never made sexual overtures toward Ms. Smith, and therefore, her employer found that their sexual harassment policy was not triggered by his actions. The employer's sexual harassment policy prohibited only "sexual harassment, sexual advances, requests for sexual favors, and other verbal or physical conduct of a sexual nature." While this policy directly tracked language from old EEOC guidelines, it did not mention discrimination based on the gender of the victim, as required by the new EEOC guidelines. Although the court found that a deficient policy does not necessarily negate an employer's affirmative defense in all cases, an out-dated policy, coupled with inaction on the part of the church, creates a strong case for liability, even though the church administration may believe it is acting in a reasonable manner.

As yours is a religious organization, consider holding your employees accountable to a more rigorous standard of conduct than the minimum prescribed by law. The biblical tenets governing your organization do preclude behavior that constitutes harassment. Therefore, in addition to setting forth a legally adequate anti-harassment plan, also stipulate that failure to abide by the organization's code of Christian conduct, or tenets of faith, constitutes grounds for discipline up to and including termination.

When you have determined that an employee has engaged in conduct that violates your church's policy, react promptly and firmly. Employers often hesitate to discipline an employee absent evidence that establishes that misconduct occurred "beyond a reasonable doubt." This is not the standard upon which disciplinary decisions are to be based. Rather you may take any employment action you deem appropriate based on your good faith understanding and belief of the facts. Moreover, if you wait until the "criminal law" standard is met before taking action, your organization may be passively promoting the type of repeated offenses that lead to civil liability.

As a final suggestion, be sure that no employees are ever led to believe that management does not want to hear about personnel problems or that all differences should be worked out internally between the parties involved. The key to defending sexual harassment claims is the maintenance of an open, "transparent" workplace where management seeks to know more, not less, about the inner workings of the organization.

PUTTING A S.T.O.P. TO CHILD ABUSE IN YOUR CHURCH

Failure to properly manage and control childcare in our churches will inevitably lead to the horror of child abuse. The foreseeable consequences include: severe emotional and psychological trauma to the young victims; shattered spiritual lives of the victims and their families; shock waves of mistrust and disillusionment throughout the congregation; fears and concerns of families associated with the victims at the realization that a child abuser typically has had multiple victims; the worst of adverse publicity that is renewed multiple times as the incident works its way through Child Protective Services, the criminal justice system, and the civil justice system; and, of course, the multimillion dollar lawsuit that may take years to be filed (the statute of limitations is tolled for minors) and may take years to conclude.

The formula for successfully dealing with the issue of child abuse in your church is S.T.O.P.:

Screen - avoid claims of negligent hiring and selection.

Train - increase awareness and avoid claims of negligent supervision.

Obey - obey abuse reporting requirements.

Prepare - to respond.

Screen - avoid claims of negligent hiring/negligent Selection

1.Screening Form

Each church must establish a workable and effective screening form to be completed by applicants for a position, whether voluntary or compensated, that involves the supervision of minors. This is not to be confused with an employment application.

The information sought by the screening form is directed to and seeks information about past church work and experience, history of abuse in the life of the applicant and information concerning prior criminal charges or convictions.

The screening form should include a release from the individual to contact references to obtain information about their character, fitness, and ability to work with children and youth. The screening application should also release the church from any liability for usage of the authorization to obtain information.

Screening application forms should also include an authorization for the church to conduct a criminal records background check.

The church should seek competent legal counsel to assist in the preparation of the screening form to comply with the laws of your particular state and in order to address any recent changes in the laws of your state.

The screening application should include a place to list references as well as previous establishments where the applicant has worked with children.

If the screening form information reveals a history that has involved incidences of child abuse, even where the applicant is or was a victim, we strongly advise that the applicant not be further considered for a position working with children and youth. If the applicant was a victim of child abuse, it is very important that the next several steps be given great attention, if the applicant is given further consideration for a position as an employee or a volunteer.

2.Contact References

Contact each reference listed on the application and make a written record of each contact. Once the references have been contacted, the notes of each contact should be kept with the screening form application and maintained in a file.

Contact each church that the applicant claims to have attended.

If churches or references listed on the screening form are reluctant to give you information regarding the applicant's prior conduct, provide them with a copy of the release that is a part of the screening form, that allows the church to obtain such information from references without legal liability.

3.Personal Interview

If an individual is applying for a position that would permit direct contact with minors, that individual should be interviewed by a member of the church staff who is schooled and skilled in screening child care and youth care workers.

4.Criminal Records Check

With an authorization set forth in the screening application form for the church to conduct a criminal records background check, one should be completed on all paid workers whose position necessarily involves the custody or supervision of minors. It is also advisable to do a criminal records check on all paid workers whose position necessarily involves incidental but routine contact with children.

If the criminal records check reveals a conviction of a sex-related crime, the individual should be disqualified for child care and youth work in the church. This is the "One Strike" Rule. There should be no second chances when children are involved. These persons may serve in other areas of the church, but must be prohibited from direct contact with children. If the criminal records check reveals a conviction of a crime of moral turpitude, it is advisable to contact the church's legal counsel for an opinion as to whether the charge or conviction should disqualify the individual for child care and youth work in the church.

By implementing these relatively simple yet effective steps, church leaders can significantly reduce the likelihood of an incident of abuse or molestation occurring by having every applicant for child care and youth work complete an effective screening application form and then following through with reference contacts and maintaining notes of each contact in the applicant's file, and where appropriate, conducting personal interviews by a qualified staff member, and conducting a criminal records check.

Lawsuit Statistics

In the past two decades, our country has seen an explosion in lawsuits against churches. In 1984, for the first time, a lawsuit was brought against a church for negligence concerning a minister who molested a child. With several thousand allegations of sexual abuse occurring annually within Protestant and Catholic churches, lawsuits are regularly being filed with the potential to bring multi-million dollar judgments or settlements. The following are some revealing statistics from various sources:

• One national study found that 27% of women and 16% of men had experienced some form of child sexual victimization.

• In 1994, state Child Protective Services agencies received an estimated two million reports of abuse and neglect involving 2.9 million children.

• In fiscal year 1996, Texas' Child Protective Services agency received and referred for investigation 99,780 reports of alleged abuse and neglect.

• In 1996, over twenty children were confirmed each day by Texas' Child Protective Services agencies as child sexual abuse victims.

• The Texas Department of Protective and Regulatory Services projects over 170,000 reports of child abuse and neglect for fiscal year 1998.

• Several thousand allegations of sexual abuse occur annually within Protestant and Catholic churches.

• Approximately 1% of all churches have been sued.

Common sense leads to the conclusion that large, fast growing churches, with many new faces and many young faces, have tremendous exposure unless action is taken to avoid or greatly reduce the risk of an incident of child abuse and particularly, child sexual abuse.

TRAIN

You have obtained a completed application with an executed background check consent form, interviewed the applicant, checked his or her references, conducted the criminal background check and everything looks good. So far, so good. Based upon your usage of an effective screening program, you have decided that the applicant is well qualified to serve as a volunteer or employee at your church. Arguably, your church has used due diligence and thereby exercised reasonable care in its selection of its church worker.

The next legal hurdle for your program is the potential claim that your church was unreasonable because it failed to supervise or train a worker and that the church's failure to supervise or train resulted in injury to a child. This claim arises most often when a non-supervisory employee or volunteer is alleged to have engaged in sexual misconduct with a child.

We recognize everyone is very busy these days. Training programs are easily relegated to the back burner when considering all the urgent things that must be done. But in the area of preventing child abuse in the church, proper training and adequate supervision of workers is critical. Training and education is an important weapon in your arsenal for putting a STOP to child abuse.

Important aspects of a training program

Your training program should minimally include the following areas:

Recognizing a Perpetrator of Child Abuse

It is important that we not paint the picture of child abuse with too broad a brush. Its causes are many, varied and complex. Stereotypes do not serve well in this arena. Child abuse can be carried out by anyone given the opportunity and who possesses the inclination.

Child abuse occurs in all types of settings by people of all races, creeds and socioeconomic and educational backgrounds. Persons known to the child perpetrate four out of five assaults on children. Children of all ages can be the victims of it. Adults are not the only perpetrators, children also victimize other children.

2. Identification of victims of child abuse

Quite often, victims of child abuse live in a world of silence. They may not understand that what they are experiencing is wrong, they may feel a sense of loyalty to the offender (especially if the molester/abuser is a family member), they may feel guilty about getting the offender in trouble, or they may feel afraid of the repercussions if they "tell." However, victims cry out for help, even if their actions are unintentional. Our responsibility is to recognize the verbal or behavioral signs of abuse so that we might rescue a child from a destructive situation.

3. Appropriate Interaction with children

Jesus clearly demonstrated that some certain forms of touching are appropriate and should be encouraged. In many cases, they can enhance a child's feeling of safety and self-worth. Mark 10:16 tells us that Jesus took little children and babies in his arms, put his hands on them and blessed them. However, other forms of inappropriate touching can cause confusion, shame, and hurt to the child subjected to it. Therefore, it is crucial that all those who work with children receive training in proper interaction.

Adequately training and equipping your childcare workers is important business. Therefore, every church must take the time to develop an ongoing training program that covers these areas. Make certain to research your options and choose a program that is user-friendly and effective.

OPERATE

Even with utilization of a proper screening program, your Church must take the next step. Courts are intolerant of childcare facilities without an operational program. However, the only thing worse than not having an operational program is implementing one and not following its rules. Failure to employ and monitor such safeguards can result in liability for negligent supervision and operation of your S.T.O.P. program. Therefore, it is crucial that you understand the laws of your state, as well as the acts and omissions that courts look for in assigning blame, should the unthinkable occur.

Proper Supervision and Operation

If your church does not adequately supervise the activities taking place within its four walls, it is opening itself up to liability. Another area of potential liability is situations in which groups go off-site, such as overnight camping excursions and missions trips. Not only should you avoid any "iffy" situations, a supervisor needs to be aware of what is taking place with the children as much as possible.

Can you be everywhere at once? Of course not. Is this a tremendous responsibility? Absolutely. And it may be time consuming. But, it is impossible to underscore the importance of awareness - knowing what is going on in your facility and with your children. Just as we would each desire to protect our own children from any harm, we should also adopt that desire for any children entrusted to our care. Therefore, there needs to be a strong system of supervision; whether the children are at the church or out on a church-sponsored activity.

Any childcare facility has two fundamental responsibilities. One is the moral responsibility. The other responsibility is legal. Because of this legal responsibility, courts will look to see if the church has been negligent, not only in its screening of volunteers and employees, but also in its care of minors.

Negligence

Churches need to have at least a cursory understanding of what their legal duties are in order to protect against the occurrence of negligence. Negligence may be thought of as acting carelessly and without proper attention. The law defines negligence as conduct that creates an "unreasonable risk of foreseeable harm" to others. Remember that churches cannot guarantee complete safety to every child in their care. Kids hurt themselves every day, regardless of how stringent the supervision. What churches must do, however, is guard against an injury that may occur as a result of their own carelessness or failure to provide proper attention.

Factors of negligence

There are essentially three components to any claim of negligence. Let's attempt to understand each.

A duty to exercise "Reasonable Care"

First, a duty of reasonable care must exist. A duty of reasonable care exists when you take on the care of children. For the most part, courts have defined "reasonable" to mean the actions an ordinary, prudent person would take under the same or similar circumstances.

A breach of the duty of reasonable care has taken place

Once it has been determined that a duty exists, then there needs to be proof that the duty was breached. This can be proven by:

an incident resulting in injury to a child, and

evidence that the church could have somehow prevented it by taking adequate safety measures (e.g., failure to supervise interaction between workers and children that results in molestation of a child).

Damages caused by that breach

If a court finds that the church breached a duty of reasonable care toward a child in their custody and care, generally, it will not be difficult for a court to find that damages were caused by the church's breach. The physical and psychological injury alone is often times enough for a court to hold the church accountable.

Two ways churches can be negligent

Church's own negligence

As stated previously, a church may be liable for its own acts of negligence. Selection of an employee that they have reason to believe is a sexual offender is an example of their own negligence. Improper supervision of activities is another example.

Vicarious liability

The theory of vicarious liability is based upon the understanding that employers are responsible for the actions of their employees/volunteers. These actions must take place while the "agent" (the volunteer or employee) is performing duties on behalf of the church.

Delegation of Duties

To maintain order and promote security, it is best to have one primary director responsible for maintaining the oversight of the operational portion of the S.T.O.P. program. If too many individuals are involved in supervising the S.T.O.P. program, things can slip through the cracks.

The following is a list of important considerations and obligations of the director of a childcare facility:

Reports to pastors and elders

The Director should conduct a regular meeting with the pastor and elders of the church. The report should contain a reminder of the safeguards implemented within the church to guard against abuse, what actions have been taken against any potential molesters, and any other information deemed necessary.

A paid staff member or long-term volunteer

If possible, the Director should be a paid staff member because this creates an extra incentive for the person to be alert and organized. Be sure to include this duty in the person's employment description and it have him sign an agreement stating that he understands its nature and responsibility.

Strategic Supervision

One of the most effective ways for the director to maintain clear oversight of activities is for her to create a policy of "Strategic Supervision." In order for the director to know what is occurring, she must be touring the facility during hours of operation. These tours should be random, without warning, and never limited to any one part of the facilities. They should encompass all areas where children are present, including closets, basements, bathrooms, etc.

While we cannot cover every potential issue, carefully screening potential childcare workers, providing them with clear instruction and training, and operating within organizational, federal and state guidelines will greatly enhance your church's ability to protect itself against child abusers. However, should the unthinkable occur, the church must be equipped with a PLAN.

PLAN TO RESPOND

THE PLAN

So, what should your church do if the unthinkable occurs? Your entire staff and congregation will be in shock; experiencing a wide range of emotions, from denial to hysteria, from fear to sorrow. This is not the time to strategize about how you should respond to a report of child abuse at your church.

By implementing a plan to respond to allegations of abuse, you can cover all of the appropriate steps. If you don't prepare yourselves in advance, it is probable that you'll act on emotion, and make unwise choices, rather than following the most advantageous path to protect the victim, the rights of the accused, and the church.

An accusation may come in the form of a concerned parent, a childcare worker who notices improper behavior, or maybe a statement made by a child. However the allegation manifests, one person, preferably the director of the children's ministries, should be given the responsibility of alerting the leader of the Response Team. Your church will want to fashion a list containing contact numbers for the leader of the Response Team and alternate persons to be contacted immediately upon receipt of a report.

The Response Team should be assembled immediately after notice has been given to supervisors so that interaction between the alleged wrongdoer can be prevented and basic information gathered from the church worker who made the report. The Response Team leader should gather this basic information.

Response to Allegation Checklist

Notify the Response Team Group Leader

Secure the safety of the child

Listen to the child

Notify the parents

Notify the authorities

Notify your attorney

Notify your insurance carrier

Remove the alleged perpetrator

Prepare a statement to the press

Maintain the privacy of all involved

The mere receipt of a report should trigger the church's efforts to prevent interaction between the alleged wrongdoer and children. Regardless of whether an accusation seems unfounded, immediately remove the accused from any position involving children. Again, don't procrastinate. This does not have to take place in a public forum. If the offender is a high church official, it may be more difficult to remove him without publicity, however, remember that this is the first critical step in the plan.

It is critical to never ignore an allegation of child abuse, no matter how unlikely it may seem. First, and possibly the most important thing your church leaders can do is to remember to take each and every reported allegation seriously. Many of the problems faced by churches in the past, such as continued abuse of children and large monetary awards levied against the institutions could have been easily avoided had the church leaders faced the problem when first reported. Instead of shuffling the offender to another position and refusing to confront the issue, had they instigated a thorough investigation and dealt with the issues, countless children might have been saved the awful pain of abuse.

Understandably, it may be difficult to believe that someone you admire and trust could ever hurt a child, especially if this person is in a position of leadership within your congregation. And, while an allegation may in fact turn out to be false, it is incumbent upon you to thoroughly investigate and report any accusations levied against any church worker, volunteer or official. Having an attitude that refuses to properly investigate the accusations because "everyone knows he would never do something like that" will endanger future children and expose your church to financial liability.

Things to do when interviewing a victim of child abuse

Attempt to obtain pertinent information from others prior to the interview, including the specifics of the abuse — the date, exact time, place, sequence of events, people present, and time lag before any report took place.

Sit near the child, not across a desk or table, and at the child's eye level.

Attempt to establish a trusting relationship.

Conduct the interview in private and without the caretaker present.

Explain the purpose of the interview to the child in language appropriate to his/her developmental level.

Use the child's own words and terms in discussing the situation whenever feasible.

Always ask the child if he/she has any questions and answer them.

Ask the child to explain words or terms that are unclear.

Acknowledge the child's feeling and emphasize that the child was not at fault.

Response Team

The Response Team should be made up of a group of leaders within your church and outside professionals who are schooled, skilled and ready to respond to the report of child abuse.

Unless an accusation is leveled against one of the following leaders, the following group of leaders should be given consideration for inclusion on the Response Team:

The Response Team Leader
The Senior Pastor
The Children's Director

The Youth Pastor: if the minor is involved in junior high or high school ministry

Attorney: You'll want to include your church's attorney in every step of this process. Again, because of the emotional nature of issues involved, it will be important to involve a person who can assist you with the legal issues involved such as reporting requirements, clergy privilege, and other issues while maintaining professional objectivity. Another advantage of involving your attorney in any investigation of abuse is that some information obtained by the attorney may be subject to the attorney/client privilege depending upon the laws of your state. As such, these communications may not be available for disclosure to any person should litigation result

Any other members in your church that you may feel have special training or ability to deal with these situations such as child psychologists, pediatric health care specialists, etc.

Notification Procedures

Notify Parents. Because the report received was about a worker of the church and not about the parent or guardian of the child victim, the Response Team Leader should immediately place a telephone call to the parents or guardian of the child victim. At that time, an in-person meeting between the Response Team Leader and Director of Children's Ministries (consider whether other Response Team members, including the attorney for the church should be present) and the parents of the child victim should be scheduled. If the report was made about the parents or guardians of the child victim, then a call would not appropriate at this juncture. Instead, the Response Team Leader should consult with the church's attorney.

Notify Accused. It will be necessary to notify the alleged wrongdoer of the receipt of the report of child abuse. Inform the alleged wrongdoer that the church is not on a witch-hunt, rather, the church is acting responsibly to a serious allegation and is on a quest to find the truth. The Church should seek to gain basic who, what, when, where, how information from the alleged wrongdoer. The interview questions should be open-ended. For example, "In your work with children, has anything happened recently in the nursery that has been unusual or out of the ordinary?" Seek to gain as much information as possible without disclosing detailed or unnecessary information.

Notify Insurance Carrier. It may seem odd to notify your insurance carrier of an allegation of abuse upon the initial receipt of a report of child abuse and before there has been a final determination. However, this may be necessary because your insurance may require immediate notification for coverage. Also, you'll need to determine whether or not the church's insurance covers sexual impropriety. Many insurance policies do not cover sexual issues because of the high risk of liability.

Notify the Authorities. Each state has its own mandatory reporting requirements. It is important to become familiar with the laws of your state and to be willing to make such reports. Failure to do so can result in criminal and civil liability. Not only can the church be damaged by such failure, but a lawsuit may also be filed against an individual who fails to follow the standards set forth by the state legislature. Very few states protect clergy from reporting suspected child abuse, so the "clergy-penitent" privilege will rarely apply. If in doubt, contact your attorney.

The sexual abuse of children is an extremely serious matter. In my experience, I have seen how abuse can destroy lives, families and churches. In one extreme instance, an abuser committed suicide upon the discovery of his molestations. Churches cannot afford to be naÔve. The price is much too high.

My goal is to equip the church with the practical and legal skills necessary to protect its innocent children. I believe, however, that in addition to the use of the STOP program, we must not lose sight of the immense power of God. As His children, we are entitled to live in peace and joy. We don't have to live in fear, worrying about what may take place tomorrow - in fact, we are commanded not to.

Counseling Programs

In the background of Church development in this country, counseling by members of the clergy as an outreach to the congregation has always been present in some form. However, in the foreground of legal development, we have seen the adoption, on a state by state basis, of various statutes and causes of action which appear to be directed toward (a) limiting the public's access to providers of counseling services and (b) providing avenues of relief for those harmed by the fault of their counselors. Over time, the traditional deference that our states have afforded to church counseling efforts may be further eroded.

Specifically, states have taken three steps in the area of regulating counseling activities that clergy members must be aware of if their communications with individuals in their congregations reach any depth beyond casual conversation.

1.States have defined by statute what they consider to be the provision of mental health services and, similarly, who is to be considered a mental health service provider.

2.States have implemented strict regulations with respect to the provision of mental health services.

3.States have recognized and fostered numerous remedies, through statute or common law, addressing malpractice issues arising in the context of the counseling services.

One Important Exception in the law

It is, of course, your obligation to familiarize yourself with the laws governing your jurisdiction, but you will probably find that but for the existence of one narrow statutory exception, the activities you engage in would otherwise necessitate the issuance of a license by your state (after you have met other requirements) and constitute the provision of mental health services by a mental health services provider. This is because the nature of the matters you are presented with as a member of the clergy, that is the disorders, symptoms, conflicts, and behaviors, of any given counselee, are not inherently different from other mental health conditions presented to any other mental health provider. Furthermore, if you allow yourself to be held out as a provider of services to people seeking any form of relief from any of these conditions, then the services you perform will be presumed to be mental health services, as the fact that you are a member of the clergy offers you no insulation in the majority of jurisdictions.

The important exception mentioned above that separates your services from those of a licensed professional counselor is the self-imposed limit you recognize and strictly abide by in responding to each issue the counselee presents. That is, the majority of courts draw a distinction between a clergy member providing religious, moral, and Biblical counseling, teaching and instruction, (spiritual counseling) and one providing assessment, diagnosis, treatment, or counseling that amounts to mental health services, as your state defines that term. Crossing this line can be dangerous for two reasons. The first reason is that most states have well-defined training and certification requirements for individuals seeking a license to perform counseling dealing with mental health and emotional well-being. Performing those services without a license violates the state's certification requirements and circumvents the state's efforts to protect the welfare of its residents through regulation, which is within its right to do. Secondly, as long as you make certain that your counseling deals specifically with spiritual issues, taking care not to stray into diagnosing or treating the problems you perceive, you help protect yourself from malpractice-related liability because matters of biblical and spiritual interpretation are traditionally protected from scrutiny by the courts.

Pastoral Counseling v. Spiritual Counseling

There is another concern worthy of attention. Pastoral counseling, and the activities engaged in by pastoral counselors, should not be confused with spiritual counseling, and the range of appropriate activities spiritual counseling implies. Pastoral counseling is different from spiritual counseling in that pastoral counselors hold themselves out to be mental health professionals who have specialized graduate level training in both religion and behavioral sciences. These counselors may be state licensed as professional counselors or licensed in a variety of areas of mental health specialization. Additionally, a separate certification process by the American Association of Pastoral Counselors exists. As a result of these distinctions, a pastoral counselor's activities should not be used as a gauge for establishing acceptable parameters for biblical counselors, as doing so may expose you to the very forms of liability this article attempts to avoid.

Finally, the following points are offered as suggestions for further protecting your Church and preventing the possibility of mistaken expectations before they arise.

FIVE R'S OF CHURCH COUNSELING

1. Release - secure a written release from each counselee acknowledging that they are seeking, and the church is providing spiritual counseling, and spiritual counseling only, and disclaiming any form of mental health, non-spiritual counseling.

2. Research - consult the laws of your state pertaining to background checks/inquiries and make inquiries to all prior employers of counseling pastors.

3. Review - the law with your staff, and their procedures and counseling activities; that is, take reasonable steps to prevent improper conduct.

4. React - immediately if it comes to your attention that a pastor may be interacting inappropriately with a counselee, or a church member in general; that is, take appropriate steps to stop inappropriate conduct and report it to the proper authorities.

5. Retain - legal counsel upon suspecting misconduct or receiving an allegation.

CONFIDENTIALITY IN THE CHURCH

Historically, the obligation of the clergy to maintain the confidentiality of information given to them by their congregation has been a moral one only. However, in recent years there have been an increased number of lawsuits brought for invasion of privacy and other tort claims arising out of the disclosure of confidential information by a pastor or other church official. The result has been a recognition that the obligation to maintain confidentiality is not only a moral obligation, but often a legal one. This obligation is not absolute, however, and churches should be aware of the impact that both the Constitution and the laws of their state have on their legal obligations of confidentiality.

Confidentiality. Confidentiality is the ethical and often legal responsibility to safeguard members of the congregation from unauthorized disclosures of information given in the context of a confidential pastor-parishioner relationship. Confidentiality refers to the duty not to disclose this information to anyone.

One consequence of improperly breaching a confidence is a suit alleging invasion of privacy. While the Constitution's protections against governmental infringement on the free exercise of religion pose significant obstacles to a successful suit against a church, it seems clear that the trend of the courts is to characterize the unauthorized disclosure as something other than religious expression in order to impose civil tort liability. Accordingly, care must be given that confidential communications are guarded by the clergy.

Invasion of privacy example.

In California, two plaintiffs filed suit against a church and several church leaders for invasion of privacy, breach of fiduciary duty, false imprisonment, emotional distress, negligent infliction of physical harm, and several other torts arising out of the disclosure of the plaintiffs' extramarital affair by the bishops of their church.

Each of the plaintiffs had confessed to one or more bishops of the church, and requested that their affair be kept confidential. Each were assured that their confessions would not be disclosed. Subsequently, one of the bishops to whom each of the plaintiffs had confessed divulged the relationship to the assembled congregation in Sunday church services. There were several other breaches of confidentiality made by leaders of the church and others, with the result being that the plaintiffs were ostracized by their families, friends, and members of the congregation.

The church and other defendants alleged that the court did not have jurisdiction over the case because the dispute was ecclesiastical in nature, and that the Constitution prevented the court from intervening in a religious dispute. The court held that the Constitution protects all religious beliefs absolutely, but only protects religious actions if certain qualifications are met.

The specific acts complained of must qualify as religious expression in order to be protected. The disclosure of confidential communications for no religious purpose would not qualify as religious expression and enjoy the possibility of constitutional immunity under the 1st Amendment. If the conduct does qualify as religious expression, the court must balance the importance to the state of the interest invaded against the burden that would result from imposing tort liability for such a claim. Even if the burden is significant, the claim will survive a motion to dismiss if the state's interests are significant, and no less restrictive burden than the possibility of eventual tort liability is available.

While the disclosure in the above case represents an extreme example, many unauthorized disclosures of confidential information can potentially give rise to liability. In fact, in 1999, the New York Supreme Court found that rabbis who disclosed information regarding communications by a divorcing congregant were not protected by the First Amendment because their actions went outside the purview of Jewish law or tradition. Courts may find that even though a burden is placed on the First Amendment rights of the church by allowing a lawsuit because of the disclosure of confidences, this burden is outweighed by the government's interest in protecting the individual.

In closing, here are some thoughts to keep in mind regarding your responsibilities:

POINTS TO PONDER

Was the communication made in the context of counseling?
If so, you must honor the confidentiality of the conversation
Make certain you clearly address the parameters of the relationship

Was the person a member of the church at the time of the communication or the disclosure?
If so, the church may be able to assert "ecclesiastical" privilege
If not, the church is more open to liability

To whom are you communicating the information?
Other pastors

Only as absolutely necessary

The church body

Discouraged, unless your church bylaws give you explicit authority to do so under church discipline

Friends, neighbors, acquaintances

Absolutely prohibited

Do your bylaws address your church's right to discipline church members?

If your church utilizes disclosure to the congregation as a form of discipline, make certain this procedure is recorded in the church's governing documents

Has the person given you written permission to discuss the communication?

Within the counseling relationship, you may want to request that the counselee give you written permission to discuss the information on a limited basis

Check your own heart — what is the reason for your disclosure?

If you're disclosing the information because you feel animosity or frustration toward the individual, you can be held liable for your actions

Don't say anything unless you can prove your actions are not based on your own emotions

The legal protection for confidential information, privilege, is a good guideline for determining what disclosures of confidential information are allowed, and perhaps even required, by law. While each state's privilege rules differ, every state has some form of privilege for communications made to a member of the clergy in the context of a confessional or penitential communication.

Privilege is the legal mechanism that prevents confidential communications from being disclosed in a court proceeding. In order for a confidential communication to be privileged, it is essential that a state statute specifically identify the communication as privileged. Privileged-communication laws ensure that disclosures of personal and sensitive information will be protected from exposure in legal proceedings. This privilege belongs to the person who disclosed the information and is designed for their protection, rather than for the protection of the clergy. If a parishioner waives this privilege, therefore, the pastor has no legal grounds for withholding the information and must disclose it upon proper request. Some other relationships that are protected in various jurisdictions in the United States include those between attorneys and clients, marital partners, physicians and patients, psychotherapists and clients, accountants and clients, and nurses and patients.

In several jurisdictions, there is also privilege for confidential communications between the patient and the mental health professional in the course of diagnosis, evaluation, or treatment. This rule applies to any person licensed or certified by the state in the diagnosis, evaluation or treatment of any mental or emotional disorder. The confidentiality extends to the professional's records as well, to protect the identity of the patient as well as the diagnosis, evaluation, and treatment.

One important exception to the privilege rules deals with the issue of suits affecting the parent-child relationship. In mental health counseling, it may be possible to uncover information that concerns a child and that is the subject of a pending lawsuit. It is this exception that makes it critical for a church that provides counseling services to distinguish what type of services they are providing and to understand the difference it makes to their congregation. If the counseling is pastoral or spiritual counseling only, the only exception in many states is for the reporting of child abuse. If the counseling is mental health counseling, the argument can be made that the exceptions of the mental health privilege would apply, and the information could be compelled by the court in a suit involving a parent-child relationship. Failure to differentiate between these could give rise to liability on the part of the church and the counselor, for example, based on the lack of informed consent, if the person being counseled is inaccurately led to believe that nothing he or she tells the pastor/counselor can ever be revealed.

Another situation in which the privilege would not apply is when the individual or someone authorized to act on his behalf signs a written waiver of the right to the privilege or confidentiality. The privilege is then eliminated and the information is subject to disclosure.

Any waiver of the privilege that is used, however, must be clear and specific, so that the person understands that anything told to the pastor/counselor will not be kept confidential if requested by a third party. This does not change the confidential nature of the communication or records, but does prevent the counselor and the counselee from claiming that they are "privileged."

As a final note, if you are confronted with a difficult situation and are in doubt about the release of information, it is sensible to consult with an attorney of your choice, who may not only be able to advise you, but may be able to obtain an agreement that protects you and your church.

CHAPTER FIVE

HOW TO EFFECTIVELY HIRE

AND MANAGE LAWYERS

Curtis W. Wallace

As your organization grows and prospers, it is unavoidable that by necessity, you will need to hire and as a result, manage lawyers and other outside professionals. This experience, like any other can prove to be mutually rewarding or equally detrimental to both sides of the equation. A great deal of the success of these relationships depends less on whether you have hired the "best lawyer in town" than on the approach that you bring to the relationship.

When working with professionals, remember a few basic rules. First, seek out and find the right person for your given situation. Most people treat lawyers or accountants as if they are one size fits all. What I mean by this is that people believe that a good lawyer can handle any given legal situation — from criminal defense to a real estate deal. To make matters worse, most lawyers perpetuate this idea. The same applies to accountants and often to other professionals such as bankers or management consultants. The reason is simple, most professionals want to get paid and, as a result, never turn down a lucrative assignment. Even fewer professionals are comfortable referring their prize clients to others who may try to "steal" the client and take over all of the client's work.

This example will illustrate an important point. Because the church world is a relatively small world and a relatively small number of lawyers represent a significant number of churches, it is fairly common for conflicts of interest to arise. For instance, two different ministries, represented by the same lawyer, become engaged in a dispute with the same vendor. Depending on the exact circumstances, one ministry may have divergent interest from the other. As a result, the lawyer for the two ministries will not be able to represent both ministries and the lawyer will have to represent one ministry or the other, but not both.

In such a case, one of the ministries will be in the position of hiring a different lawyer to represent it in the dispute. When this happens, a couple of competing interests need to be balanced. As a client, you want a lawyer who will do a great job representing your interest. What you do not want is a lawyer whose sole interest is in stealing you as a client. Be wary of the lawyer who spends all of his or her time criticizing the work of your regular lawyer. Remember that lawyers are trained and are in the business of "spin" and the art of argument. In addition, there are often many ways to achieve a desired legal result. As a result, it is very easy for one lawyer to criticize another lawyer's work.

The point is simple. While it is unwise not to listen to counsel, it is also unwise to judge your lawyer based on a single criticism. Instead, evaluate both lawyers based on their body of work. In addition, make sure that credibility and integrity are major elements in your evaluation.

Understanding How Lawyers Work

In order to gain some understanding of what you should look for in a lawyer, you need some background on how lawyers work and how the practice of law has developed over time. A hundred years ago, the practice of law was such that most lawyers practiced in individual offices and handled all of their clients various legal matters. One lawyer would handle any problem a client had. Today, the reality is that lawyers, like doctors, have had to change their method of practice. The law is ever expanding and grows more complex with each passing day. As a result, lawyers, like doctors, have evolved into two levels of practice.

On one level is the traditional general practice lawyer. This lawyer handles a variety of cases and matters and has a limited knowledge of a multitude of practice areas. For instance, the general practice lawyer may handle some lawsuits, some real estate matters, divorces, basic business transactions, estate matters and some criminal cases. This lawyer takes on the cases that his clients bring, as long as he or she feels competent to handle the matter. In this way, the general practice lawyer is very much like your family physician. He or she can typically identify your problem and, in many cases, help you resolve the problem.

The weakness of the general practice lawyer is that he or she cannot know everything about everything and may not have a specific expertise that you need. Therefore, like your family doctor, a general practice lawyer will take care of 95% of what ails you. However, it is that other 5% that you need to worry about.

Because of the inability of the general practice lawyer to keep pace with the growing complexity of the law in every area, a second tier of lawyers has developed. These lawyers focus their practice on very narrow areas of the law in which they can develop a high level of expertise, knowledge and connections. Just as a doctor may devote his entire career performing heart surgery, a lawyer may spend his career advising clients only on tax matters. These lawyers, like medical specialists, are equipped to handle the most complex and unusual matters that may arise in the course of your organization's evolution.

Specialist lawyers work in a variety of settings. Most tend to work within large firms that are made up of lawyers with diverse specialties. Other specialists work alone or within small firms made of lawyers with the same or related specialties. These specialty or "boutique" firms usually receive a lot of their business in the form of referrals from firms that do not have a lawyer with that particular specialty.

Large law firms, on the other hand, are built on the idea that one firm, with lawyers who specialize in a number of complimentary practice areas, can meet the diverse needs of various clients. This model combines the convenient "one-stop-shopping" of the general practice lawyer with the advantage of getting a specialist to handle each matter, regardless of the area of law involved.

At first blush, large law firms appear to be the ideal solution. You only need one law firm and every problem is handled by an expert in that area. However, the structure of these large law firms also creates a few significant disadvantages. First, because the individuals in the firms are specialists, they tend to be much more expensive than general practice lawyers. For example, partners in such firms often charge in the range of $300 to $500 per hour, plus expenses. Even associates (associates are the younger lawyers who do not yet own a portion of the firm but are instead employees of the firm) commonly charge in the range of $150 to $300 per hour, depending on their experience level. By comparison, even a senior partner in a general practice with 20 years of experience will probably only charge in the $175 to $250 per hour, depending on the city.

An additional disadvantage of some large law firms is that some such firms will not even accept your organization as a client unless they expect you to give them a certain amount of work per year. For example, some major law firms do not want clients who will not generate a minimum of $25,000 to $50,000 per year in billings. The reason is simple, these firms primarily cater to America's corporate heavyweights who generate millions per year in legal work. It simply is viewed as unprofitable to allocate resources to a client that can generate only a limited amount of work.

In addition, because most of the lawyers in these large law firms are specialist, it is often difficult to get one lawyer in the firm with whom you can develop a long-term relationship. In my opinion, it is critical to have a good solid relationship with at least one lawyer who can not only solve specific problems, but act as a general counselor and advisor to your organization. In order to act in that role, a lawyer needs to have a good overall understanding of your activities and organizational structure. It is difficult for a specialist who only works for you on sporadic matters limited to his or her area of expertise to accumulate the necessary institutional knowledge about your ministry.

Without the benefit of a lawyer with in-depth institutional knowledge of your organization, you will either spend inordinate amounts of time bringing different lawyers up to speed of your activities or you will have something critical missed. More than likely, you will have something missed. The reason is simple. If your ministry is very large, it is likely that multiple people in your ministry will have contact with lawyers. That contact will relate to their specific area of responsibility. Moreover, the person in your ministry dealing with the lawyers probably does not know everything about your organization. So, if your representative does not have full knowledge and the lawyer does not have full knowledge, the advise that you get will be issue specific but may not take into account some valuable piece of information.

For this reason, you need to be sure that you have at least one lawyer who has a thorough knowledge of your ministry and its activities and objectives. A lawyer with a wide knowledge will save you tens of thousands of dollars in legal fees. How is that possible? It is possible because lawyers usually charge by the hour. When a lawyer with a deep knowledge of your ministry gives you advise in a ten minute phone call that would have taken another lawyer five hours (because that lawyer would have to ask questions and gather information), you have saved at least a thousand dollars.

Therefore, my suggestion is to be aware of and utilize a multitude of counsel. Both law firm models discussed above have rightful places. At the outset, your organization needs a good general practice lawyer. He or she will act as your family physician treating the occasional illness and, hopefully, dispensing quality advice on healthy living. While they are relatively rare, it is wise to seek out a lawyer who has some experience with either church specifically or non-profit organizations in general. Each of the lawyers who contributed to this book are excellent examples of lawyers who have developed expertise dealing with churches and ministries. While church law itself has not yet really developed into a specific practice specialty that is represented in the large law firms, there are lawyers, such as those represented in this book, in smaller general practice firms who have experience with many of the unique issues encountered by churches and other non-profits.

If you cannot find a suitable lawyer with church experience, remember that your church is a non-profit corporation, just like the United Way or The Boy Scouts, a university, or some hospitals. Therefore, a lawyer who has experience with other types of non-profits will likely understand the core issues faced by your ministry, even though he or she may not have notable experience with a church specifically.

Then, as your organization grows and prospers, your needs will become increasingly complex. As your needs change, you will need to expand your legal base to include specialists in different areas. For example, large churches all have one thing in common, the need for a large sanctuary. Buying an existing small church build-ing or building a $3,000,000 building is one thing. The planning and construction of a $40,000,000 facility is something entirely different. It would be the rare general practice lawyer who is quali-fied to negotiate a $40,000,000 construction contract with a major contractor and negotiate and close a $25,000,000 credit facility with a national bank. It that scenario, you need someone with extensive experience working on such deals.

Similarly, if your church decides to engage in any activity in the entertainment business, whether it is as simple as an artist contract with a record company or a first-time book deal, or as complex as forming a record label and producing music, you need to obtain specialized advice. The entertainment business, both in the Christian and secular marketplaces, is one of the most shark-infest-ed realms that you can delve into. Entertainment companies have been taking advantage of amateurs for all of history. If you do not arm yourself, you are likely to become someone's lunch.

The problem with this dual-pronged strategy for using lawyers is knowing when to go get specialized help. Hopefully, you have chosen a wise and competent lawyer who is ethical enough to lead you to get specialized help when you need it. If not, the burden will be on you to know when to seek outside help.

In order to know when you have reached that point, you need to know your regular lawyer. Over time, you should obtain a sense of his or her character. In addition, you should also obtain a sense for what he or she is good at. Just as with your employees, it is critical to become comfortable with the skills and limitations of your lawyer. Don't be afraid to continually reevaluate your lawyer and his or her qualifications. Ask questions. Has she ever done this before. Make them be specific. Have the lawyer tell you about the case, about the amounts of money involved and ask to talk to other clients.

The process of learning your lawyer begins at the outset of the relationship. Interview potential lawyers as if you were hiring any other employee. I cannot tell you how many times a new client who I did not know and who did not know me, simply dropped a very important matter into my lap and followed my advice, without ever finding out what I could really do. Hopefully, I lived up to the expectations of those trusting clients. However, I was always struck by how much faith those people placed in me solely on the basis of my reputation or a referral from another client.

While lawyers naturally do not encourage it, you should feel free to interview prospective lawyers and ask very difficult questions. In addition, talk to other clients of the lawyer. Both good and bad reputations spread quickly and it is usually easy to track down a lawyer's reputation in your area. If a prospective lawyer gives the impression that he or she does not have time or is offended by the process, you are talking to the wrong lawyer. I can assure you that when lawyers go looking for counsel to handle a particular matter for them, they interview and go through the steps I have suggested.

In the course of the interview, explain your organization, its size and challenges and get the lawyer to explain their relevant expertise. Find out where the lawyer went to school. How well did the lawyer do in school. While the quality of the lawyer's legal education is, of course, not completely indicative of the quality of the lawyer, it can be helpful. For example, most large law firm rarely hire lawyers who did not graduate in the top 10-15% of their class. Success in law school typically will equate to a lawyer with a very good technical understanding of the law. As a result, most highly successful students gravitate toward careers as specialist. If you need a specialist, such as a tax lawyer, I would tend to stay away from lawyers with less than stellar academic backgrounds.

On the other hand, if you need a trial lawyer because you have been sued, then you need a lawyer who is part performer and part gunfighter. A trial involves the telling of story in an adversarial setting. Therefore, you need to find someone who will take up your cause and fight for you. Some of the best trial lawyers barely made it through law school, but they know how to fight. Remember, a lawsuit is a street fight and you need to hire accordingly.

You should keep a couple of important points in mind as you hire a lawyer. First, one very important question is who will be your point of contact in the law firm and who will do most of your work. You need to make sure that you meet both the lawyer who is your point of contact and the lawyer who will actually do most of the work for you. Most successful firms have one or more rainmakers who are primarily responsible for bringing in new business. These rainmakers are often very experienced, very smooth, very impressive salesmen who rarely, if ever, actually do any real legal work. Their task is solely to generate new client relationships and manage those relationships. Therefore, when the work comes into the firm, it is typically delegated to a younger less experienced lawyer. The moral is be careful if you are selecting a firm solely because you were very impressed by the senior partner. The key is to be impressed by both the lawyer who gets your work and the person who is doing the work.

A second related point is the accessibility of the lawyers that you choose. By definition, most good lawyers are in demand and are very busy people. However, your lawyer cannot do you any good if you do not have ready access to him or her and cannot get timely responses. Therefore, while you want a lawyer who is in demand, you also want a lawyer who is wise enough to limit his or her practice enough to allow him or her to responsibly service all of their clients.

For obvious reasons, the extent to which your lawyer is over-burdened is difficult to judge prior to your becoming a client. It will likely take time to see how available he or she is to you. Most lawyers naturally make an extra effort with new clients so it may take until the honeymoon period is over to determine how your lawyer will do. However, pay attention to the small signs. How long does it take the lawyer to return your phone calls (it should be 24 hours or less). Does every communication with your lawyer get filtered through a paralegal or secretary. I would suggest that you start looking for a new lawyer if you know his or her assistant better than you know the lawyer. Lawyers who are too busy to ade-quately service their clients frequently push too much work onto their assistants. The only communications that you should be hav-ing with your lawyer's assistant should be concerning logistical and informational matters. The assistant should be the one setting up the conference call, or calling to ask for a copy of a document or answering a simple factual question such as has a certain act been completed, etc. What should not be accepted is a back and forth dialogue with the assistant where you are having to ask the assistant your question and then waiting for the assistant to ask the lawyer and call you back. There is simply too much potential to lose valuable information in the translation and a lawyer who heavily relies on such a process should probably not be trusted to convey correct advice.

Once you have identified a quality lawyer with whom you have a rapport, develop a relationship. Involve that lawyer in your affairs to the extent that you can. It is very difficult to counsel a client in a vacuum. A good lawyer needs to know the big picture of your organization in order to fully and properly understand how a specific matter may affect other elements of the organization.

The next major issue involving the management of lawyers is the subject of costs. For the most part, lawyers bill in three ways. The most basic and common form of billing is straight hourly fee. In this scenario, the lawyer bills the client for the actual amount of time he or she spent working on the particular matter. The time spent is multiplied by the lawyer's hourly rate to determine the bill.

The next method is percentage fees. Typically used by plaintiff's lawyers representing a victim in a personal injury case, this involves the lawyer billing for an amount equal to the amount he or she wins for you in the case. Percentage billing is sometimes also used by some lawyers in the entertainment business who bill clients for a percentage of the deal obtained (in this circumstance the lawyer is acting more like an agent or manager than a pure lawyer).

The third way that lawyers bill their clients is flat-rate billing. In this scenario, a lawyer bills a client for a set amount to complete a specified task. For instance, you and your lawyer may agree that he or she will handle a certain real estate deal from start to finish for a flat fee of $25,000. In a related format, some lawyers charge monthly retainers that entitle you to certain legal services during that month.

The arrangement that you and your lawyer should settle on depends on the circumstances and negotiations. Generally, the fairest billing method is straight hourly billing. The lawyer gets paid for the time that he or she spends working for you.

With percentage billing, the lawyer often ends up with a much higher hourly fee. This may or may not represent a good deal for you, the client. For instance, you may be looking for a book deal. A good lawyer/book agent may charge you 10-20% of the value of the deal. That lawyer may only spend 20 hours getting you a deal for a $100,000 advance and earn $20,000, or $1,000 per hour. However, you are buying that lawyer's contacts and knowledge. If you could have gotten that same deal on your own (you knew who to call and what you were worth), then you have overpaid. You should have hired an hourly lawyer to simply review the contract, not to get the deal. However, if you could not get the deal on your own, the lawyer was a great deal.

The same applies to lawsuits. Your church may have a damage claim against someone. Your lawyer may be willing to take the case for a percentage of what he or she gets you. This may or may not be a good deal. If you can afford to pay hourly fees, you may get a better deal. The problem is that you do not know going in how long the case will last or how much the fees will be. Accordingly, you may want to share the risks and rewards with your lawyer. The winners and losers are determined by the outcome of the case. If it settles quickly for big money, your lawyer wins. If it goes to trial and you lose the case, the lawyer is out the legal fees.

The good and bad of the percentage approach is that you become partners with your lawyer. As settlement discussions start, you and your lawyer may have different opinions, depending on how risk averse each party is and what their objectives are. For instance, you may be angry with the party you are suing and want to prove a point by holding out for trial. Your lawyer, on the other hand, may want to settle quickly to get paid.

Similar logic applies with regard to monthly retainers and flat fee billing. Lawyers typically try to insure that they are on the right side of such arrangements. The lawyer knows better than you what is required to handle a certain matter and can set his fees accordingly. The lawyer will typically build some leeway into the fee in case things take longer than expected. This means that most flat fees are higher than corresponding hourly fees would be. However, as the client, you may want to know that the fee will not exceed a certain amount. In such cases, a flat fee may make sense.

Regardless of the billing arrangement, remember this — the client, that is you, always makes the decisions. Your lawyer cannot settle a case or agree to contract terms without your consent. If your lawyer tries to say that he has such rights or puts such rights in your attorney-client contract, get a new lawyer and call the local bar association. A lawyer cannot substitute his view for that of the client. To do so is improper and unethical.

Managing Lawyers

Once you have found a qualified lawyer and you have entered into an agreement that specifies how your lawyer will be paid, it is time to build a relationship with and manage your lawyer. This is the point where most clients run into trouble. Too often, clients will put up with sub-par service, a lack of accessability, sloppy billing practices and a lack of accountability. Remember, you are paying first class prices and you are entitled to first class service. If you do not get it, move on. Your legal matters are far too important to settle for mediocre legal representation.

With that in mind, here is this author's version of a client's Bill of Rights. Having been both a practicing lawyer and a consumer of legal services from some of the best in the business (each contributor to this book has provided legal services for this author), I am uniquely qualified to speak on the topic of legal services.

A Client's Bill of Rights

1. The client shall set the objectives of the representation and make all business decisions involved in the representation.

2. The client is entitled to a full discussion and explanation of any legal strategy proposed by his or her lawyer.

3. The client is entitled to prompt and responsive representation. All client phone calls should be returned by the lawyer within 24 hours.

4. The client is entitled to regular progress reports on all pending matters.

5. The client is entitled to an honest assessment of the time required to complete a task and an adherence to reasonable deadlines.

6. The client is entitled to clear, detailed and accurate billing.

7. The client is entitled to complete confidentiality of all information learned by the lawyer during the representation.

8. The client is entitled to full disclosure from the lawyer of all settlement offers and contract proposals.

9. The client is entitled to full disclosure of any potential con-

flicts of interest that the lawyer may have.

10. The client is entitled to integrity and honesty from the lawyer.

If your lawyer complies with this Bill of Rights, you will have good, honest, responsive legal representation. A more detailed discussion of the points in the Bill of Rights is in order.

The client shall set the objectives of the representation and make all business decisions involved in the representation.

Too often, the attorney-client relationship is misunderstood. The client is in charge and the client should make the decisions. The lawyer works for the client — not the other way around. Possibly because of the mystery surrounding the law and the special knowledge that lawyers possess, many clients act as if their lawyers should not be second guessed or even questioned. In fact, some clients want their lawyer to make business decisions for them. That is not the lawyer's place.

The lawyer's job is to provide insight into the mysterious world of the law. The lawyer should provide information and options. It is the job of the client to take the lawyer's advice, put that advice together with his knowledge and make a decision. Consider your lawyer's counsel carefully, but do not give away your right to control your own business. Your lawyer will appreciate your involvement.

2. The client is entitled to a full discussion and explanation of any legal strategy proposed by his or her lawyer.

This is very simple, if you do not understand something — ASK. Your lawyer should be able to explain every line of a contract or the reasoning behind a legal strategy. If your lawyer cannot adequately explain something, it may be because he or she does not understand it. If your lawyer prepares a document for you, but cannot explain it, you may have a problem. The lawyer may be out of his or her depth.

On the other hand, you should not to expect your lawyer to know everything about everything. The law is constantly changing and evolving. Therefore, it is OK if your lawyer says he or she does not know or understand something. There are many unanswered questions in the law. As a result, one of the real skills that a lawyer can possess is the ability to analyze a situation, do legal research, and give sound advice based on that research and analysis. In fact, it is the lawyer who always shoots from the hip and always has the answer on his tongue that is more of a problem.

3.The client is entitled to prompt and responsive representation. All client phone calls should be returned by the lawyer within 24 hours.

A lawyer who is constantly unavailable to you is not an asset. You need to be able to speak with your lawyer to address your matter. Everyone wants a good lawyer and all good lawyers are very busy people. However, you are just as busy. If your lawyer is too busy to return phone calls, he is probably too busy to properly handle your matter.

An additional point should be made here. Contact with a non-lawyer legal assistant or secretary should not substitute for contact with your lawyer. A legal assistant's job is to aid the lawyer and expedite logistical matters, such as assembling information and coordinating actions. The legal assistant should not be giving advice. Likewise, the assistant should not be taking your question, talking to the lawyer and responding back to you. Too much can be lost in the translation. In addition, the legal assistant may not ask an important question and the lawyer may give an answer based on incomplete information. Nothing will substitute for direct lawyer to client contact.

4. The client is entitled to regular progress reports on all pending matters.

This item is closely related to point three. You need to know what is going on and what the status is of each matter. This goes directly to the heart of lawyer management. You, as the client, are in charge of the relationship. You need to insist on and get regular updates. Without this information, you cannot properly manage your lawyer. He or she will end up managing your business according to the lawyer's schedule, not yours.

5. The client is entitled to an honest assessment of the time required to complete a task, adherence to reasonable deadlines and consultation before the lawyer agrees to or requests any delay.

Some lawyers take advantage of the mysterious nature of the law to put off clients and take far too long to accomplish relatively quick tasks. Even the most detailed and lengthy contracts can be prepared or reviewed in a matter of days, not weeks. Extended delays are due to something other than the time required to complete the task at hand.

With regard to lawsuits, certain timing issues are out of your lawyer's hands and in the hands of the judge. However, the judge's influence is limited to matters that require court appearances. Your lawyer has control over when items are filed with the court, when depositions are taken and the like. You should see regular activity in your case. If a month passes without action, there may be a problem. Do not be afraid to request a proposed timeline from your lawyer. Once you have it, monitor compliance.

With regard to delays, lawyers are frequently quick to agree to a request for delay by the opposing lawyer. Lawyers do this for a couple of reasons. First, they may need a similar favor in the future from the opposing lawyer and it is helpful to have people "owe you one." This can benefit your case in some cases and so you may want to agree to a delay if it does not harm your case. The point is that you should be asked.

Next, your lawyer may agree to a delay because he or she is too busy already and the delay takes one more critical item off of his or her to do list. Again, this may benefit you. You want your lawyer to be ready and prepared and the delay may accomplish that. However, you should be asked and your agreement sought.

6. The client is entitled to clear, detailed and accurate billing.

This point is simple, but critical. Each month, your lawyer should send you a statement. That statement should be easy to understand; clearly detailing the work performed by each lawyer working on your case. The bill should show each action taken by the lawyer, the time spent on the action and the amount owed. The bill should also detail the prior balance owed, if any, and the status of any retainer or prepaid fees.

You should examine bills closely, especially at the beginning of an attorney-client relationship. Your lawyer's bills will disclose a great deal about the lawyer. Here are a few things to look for:

Request that your lawyer clarify vague items such as "research" or "file work"

Find out what the lawyer was working on or researching

Request explanations for extended conferences that involve multiple lawyers in the same firm. Strategy sessions are important and invaluable, but can also hide bill padding.

Lawyers love to travel in packs. Law firm partners frequently bring along a younger associate for meetings and hearings. In most cases, this will benefit you. Associates bill at much lower rate than partners. If your lawyer properly uses his or her associates, the associates will do much of the day-to-day work on your matter, keep in contact with you and keep the case moving. Therefore, having the associate at meetings is often necessary to keep him or her up to speed. Your legal bills should reflect this activity. If you are always billed for two lawyers at every meeting, the bills should reflect two lawyers working the case. However if your bill reflects that only the partner works the case, you need to question why the associate is at the meetings.

Carefully review bills for travel charges and time spent while traveling. Hopefully, your attorney-client contract specifies what type of flights your lawyer will take (coach or first class) and the level of hotels to be used. You should expect to pay for full fare tickets because lawyers are busy and frequently change travel plans. However, it is OK to ask to make the arrangements for hotel, etc.

The tricky point is billing for time spent traveling. There are no set rules on this point. However, you should expect reasonableness. Some lawyers will bill the entire time they are traveling. That is clearly unreasonable. You should expect to pay for time that the lawyer could have spent billing another client. Here is an example. It will probably take your lawyer's entire day to take a one hour flight to see you, meet with you for two hours and then return home. Even though the lawyer only spent two hours with you, it is acceptable for your lawyer to bill you for the eight hours he could have spent working on other matters.

Before moving on, one final note about lawyer billing. Many lawyers like to charge up-front non-refundable retainers. The idea is that you pay the lawyer say, $30,000 up-front. The lawyer will then bill against the $30,000 retainer as he or she does work for you. In reality, these retainers are simply up-front advance payment of fees. The up-front nature of the fee is not in itself objectionable. Often times, the client's credit worthiness or payment history dictates such an arrangement.

The objectionable part is the non-refundable nature of the fee. While there is no legal prohibition against such fee structures, three points of legal ethics are relevant. First, a lawyer is required to maintain a trust account to hold all funds that belong to a client or have not been earned by the lawyer. A lawyer cannot mix his money and your money. This is the biggest no-no there is in legal ethics. Some lawyers take the position that a non-refundable fee is fully earned on payment (because it is non-refundable) and, as a result, the lawyer places the fee in his account, not the trust account.

Secondly, it is a rule of legal ethics that a client should always be free to hire and fire lawyers at will. For example, it is unethical for a lawyer to sign a contract that requires you to be a client for a certain length of time. You must always be free to go elsewhere if you are unsatisfied with the service you receive. An argument can be made that non-refundable fee arrangements tie you to a lawyer if you cannot afford to give up the unearned portion of the advance fee and still go hire another lawyer.

Finally, in the event of a fee dispute, your lawyer is supposed to hold the disputed money in trust while the dispute is resolved. A lawyer is prohibited from placing disputed funds in his or her account. How can the lawyer do that if he has already placed all of the money in his account. In addition, you have lost leverage in the dispute. For these reasons, I urge you to avoid such fees arrangements.

7.The client is entitled to complete confidentiality of all information learned by the lawyer during the representation.

The attorney-client privilege and the attorney's duty of confidentiality are two very serious issues. They are also different concepts. Under his duty of confidentiality, your lawyer is required to maintain the confidentiality of all information that you provide or that he or she learns about you in the course of the representation. It does not matter if the information is available from other sources. If the lawyer got the information from you, he or she must keep it confidential, unless you agree otherwise. This is the lawyer's duty to you, as a client, and is separate from the attorney-client privilege.

Under an attorney's duty of confidentiality, your lawyer should not be talking about you to others. This is particularly a problem with regard to law firm marketing. It is fine for your lawyer to list you as a representative client and to list you as a reference. However, the lawyer should not discuss your business with anyone without your consent. If your lawyer tells you too much about other clients, he is probably talking about you too.

While a lawyer's duty of confidentiality is personal to the client, the attorney-client privilege deals with when an attorney can be compelled to disclose information about you to a court. As a general matter, an attorney cannot be compelled to disclose any confidential communication between you and your lawyer. You need to understand the requirements and limits of the privilege. First, for information to be subject to the privilege, it must be a confidential communication between you and your lawyer. If you disclose the confidential information to anyone other your lawyer, it is no longer confidential and is no longer subject to the privilege. For instance, if someone else is in the room when you talk with your lawyer, the information you convey will not be privileged.

Most of the exceptions to the privilege have to do with criminal behavior or information that leads the lawyer to believe that you may harm someone in the future. Such exceptions need not be discussed here.

However, you do need to understand an important concept with regard to corporations. When a lawyer represents a corporation, he represents the entity, not the individuals that are part of the organization. As a result, the lawyers duty of confidentiality and the attorney-client privilege run to the corporation, not to the individual. The attorney's duty is to look out for the best interest of the corporation. Therefore, the lawyer may have to go to a higher authority in the corporation if he or she feels that an action of an individual would harm the corporation. This mean that if a lawyer thinks an officer is harming the church, the lawyer should go up the food chain to make the church aware of what is happening.

8. The client is entitled to full disclosure from the lawyer of all settlement offers and contract proposals.

If your lawyer is representing you in a contract negotiation or a lawsuit, you are entitled to be made aware of any and all offers made by the opposing side. The reason is simple, you control all business decisions. You cannot do that if your lawyer does not pass along offers to you. It is improper for your lawyer to decline a proposal before discussing it with you.

9.The client is entitled to full disclosure of any actual or potential conflicts of interest that the lawyer may have.

It is central to the attorney-client relationship that your attorney be focused on your best interest. That becomes difficult when your lawyer is also representing someone else who may have differing interest from your own. When your lawyer learns of a potential conflict, he or she should advise you of the circumstances so that you can make a decision about having the lawyer continue in the representation. In most cases, the potential for actual conflict is minor and you may choose to go forward. However, if a potential conflict becomes an actual conflict — the lawyer is representing two parties in the same matter on different sides — the lawyer may have to discontinue representing one or both clients.

The law of conflicts is very complicated and would take this entire book to discuss in any great detail. However, the main point is that you should be made aware of the conflict and given the opportunity to evaluate the circumstance. When looking at a potential conflict, use your common sense. Do you want this lawyer representing you if he or she is also dealing with the other party.

The downside of continuing forward when a potential conflict exists is that you may end up changing lawyers. Making a change mid-stream always cost money. You will need to pay the new lawyer to get up-to-speed on the matter; something that you have already paid to have your existing lawyer do. It is always easier to change lawyers earlier rather than later. On the other hand, if no actual conflict develops, you will not need to make a change at all. You just need to balance the information that you have.

10.The client is entitled to integrity and honesty from the lawyer.

This point needs no explanation. If you can't trust your lawyer, who can you trust. Despite all of the jokes, law is meant to be an honorable profession. Most lawyers are competent and possess the integrity that you should be seeking. Once you have found such a lawyer, develop a relationship and move forward together.

By insisting that your lawyer follow the guidelines set out above, the foundation of a mutually beneficial relationship will be established. To solidify the relationship, you will need to keep up your part of the bargain. This means that you will pay your bills in a timely manner. More importantly, you need to provide full and complete information to your lawyer. You cannot give him or her part of the picture and then expect a complete answer.

CHAPTER SIX

TAKE YOUR MINISTRY TO THE WORLD!
VIA HOLLYWOOD

Thomas G. Gehring

And

Ted Baehr

After the wildly popular Ben Hur (1957) had played in theaters all over Iran, a missionary commented that it had done more to make the crucifixion of Jesus real to Moslems than all the efforts of missionaries for the previous 150 years. Moslems believe Jesus was not crucified, and this can slow things down a bit when you try to share with a Moslem friend how much Jesus loves you and how He saved you. But, after Ben Hur, it was much easier. They had experienced the crucifixion through the powerful cinematography at the foot of the cross — nearly 100 years after General Lew Wallace had written Ben Hur, a Tale of The Christ.

A Tale of The Christ Ö has God put any Christ stories into you or your people? What are you doing to cultivate those stories, those ideas, music, or other creative endeavors? We believe there is a "woe is me if I preach not the gospel" message burning in the souls and spirits of Christians everywhere, to be expressed through powerful music, or compelling books, or high drama, or brilliant cinema that will change millions of lives all over the world.

In the mid 1990s, Robert Rodriguez (Spy Kids) cracked Hollywood with El Mariachi, a movie he wrote, directed, filmed, and produced himself with a borrowed camera and a budget within two inches of zilch. The actors were his friends. He borrowed locations, equipment, and props. He was a genius at improvisation and ... Columbia Pictures bought it, launching him on his career!

Computer animator and storyteller Phil Vischer did the same low-budget thing with Veggie Tales. He had little capital and no connections. But he had one great idea: that children's entertainment could do more than sell toys - it could positively impact lives! Working with two young art school grads and friends volunteering on weekends, he set to work in his spare bedroom on his computer and started designing Veggie Tales. Phil completed the first half-hour episode of Veggie Tales, Where's God When I'm S-Scared? before Christmas, 1993. It was the nation's first entirely computer animated video. By 2001, over 20 million Veggie Tales videos had been sold!

Has the Good News of Jesus Christ set ablaze a fire within you or your people that you should — that you must! — take to the world through music, dramatic writing, theatrical plays. or other forms, so that the creative genius He has birthed in you comes to life? Look around, it's happening, and you are called to be a part of it.

For years we have played a very active role in recruiting and encouraging a rapidly-growing group of talented professionals dedicated to making Jesus Christ known in every corner of our mission field, the entertainment industry. We love our mission field! The entertainment industry extends worldwide, but so does the Great Commission: "Go ye into all the world and preach the gospel to every creature." If God speaks to you about joining us as you read this chapter, consider that your invitation. God is telling you to join us! "Go ye,..." get your God idea out there. There are souls to be saved.

Allow us to be your guides on a short, inside tour of the U.S. entertainment industry, based in, controlled and personified by Hollywood, the part of our mission field we know best: Is the Good News Impacting Hollywood?

Consider the following upbeat reports from Dr. Baehr's book, The Media-Wise Family, listing what God did in just the first 12 years of our ministry, starting in 1985:

A major movie studio released a G-rated movie aimed at teenagers (The Princess Diaries) for the first time in thirty years.

An ever-increasing number of television and movie producers are consulting with us on their scripts and, following our advice, rewriting them to appeal to a broader audience.

A TV network and several top Hollywood producers and talent continue to meet to strategize producing more family films.

Many top executives and producers have met with us to learn more about Christian-audience movies and programs.

To help encourage more godly movies and TV programs, Sir John Templeton appointed The Christian Film and Television Commission to present the cash Epiphany Prizes for the "Most Inspiring Movie" and the "Most Inspiring TV Program."

The chairman of DreamWorks asked us to put together a theological board of advisors for its big-budget animated movie about Moses, called The Prince of Egypt. Many other producers and studios have asked us to do the same.

Thirty-six NC-17 and R-rated movies with extreme deviant sexual content were released in 1995. They earned an average of $900 thousand at the box office in an industry where it now costs $76 million to produce and release the average movie. In other words, they bombed big time at the box office, much to the surprise of Hollywood executives but not to the vast majority of Americans who abhor perverse sex.

By contrast, for many years, family movies have made much more money at the Box office than R-rated fare. For instance, in 1996, family-friendly movies grossed on average 300% better than movies aimed at the adult marketplace. In 1995, G-rated movies grossed 250% more than R-rated movies.

From 1996 to 2000, during the height of the MOVIEGUIDE Awards Gala and the Report to the Entertainment Industry, the number of movies with at least some positive moral content has risen from 87 movies in 1996 to 179 in 2000, an increase if 106%. During that same period, the number of movies with at least some positive redemptive and/or Christian content has risen from 77 in 1996 to 118 in 2000, an increase of 53%.

Many Hollywood executives and talent are coming to know JESUS Christ as Lord and Savior and are going or returning to the church.

A growing number of committed Christians are occupying positions of power and influence in the top echelons of the entertainment industry. Of the more than 45 executive producers of the sixty prime time entertainment TV programs, 23 of them were outspoken Christians in 1994, up from only one 12 years earlier.

A number of recent movies, such as The Prince of Egypt, Return To Me, Ever After, The Winslow Boy, The Patriot, The Preacher's Wife, The Spitfire Grill, Independence Day, Richard III, Braveheart,

Sense and Sensibility, The Feast of July, Persuasion, First Knight, and Cry the Beloved Country, presented the Gospel, extolled Jesus Christ, commended the Bible, and commended church. This is a significant change from years past.

In 1996, 60% of the most-profitable movies had Christian or biblical themes and elements and earned a total of $2.3 billion with total budgets of $265 million for an earnings ratio of nine to one. By contrast, none of the least-profitable movies in 1996 received a positive acceptability rating from MOVIEGUIDE. Sixty percent of these least-profitable movies were R-rated and earned an average of $7 million each while they cost an average of $23 million each to produce. "It's scary," one top studio executive said. Another commented, "I don't know what the lessons are here, except we're making a lot of movies that people don't want to see."

Doors to the most important offices in Hollywood have been opened, and evidence mounts that a powerful sea change is occurring in the entertainment industry at the very highest levels.

How the Movies Went from Exemplary to Abhorrent

In 1933, the Roman Catholic Legion of Decency (with massive boycott power) had been established to do something about the extremely low moral caliber of many Hollywood movies during the 1920s and early 1930s. Joined in 1948 by the Protestant Film Commission (called Fort Hollywood), they were able to help Hollywood hold to fairly reasonable standards of decency until 1966.

This golden period from 1933 to 1966 saw the production of many high quality films, as well as a number of Bible-based films. The Ten Commandments saved Paramount from bankruptcy, as did Ben Hur for MGM. Dr. Baehr documents a sad series of events from 1959 through 1966, when the National Council of Churches effectively shut down Fort Hollywood and concludes:

A few months after the Protestant Film Commission was shut down, Anton LaVey opened up a Church of Satan film office. Soon thereafter a plethora of political groups, from the Gay-Lesbian Task Force to radical feminists, opened up film offices to lobby the entertainment media for their points of view. After 2,000 years of fulfilling the Great Commission to go into all the world, the church halted, turned around and effectively abandoned the most powerful communications center in the world to unregenerate paganism.Ö The result has been disastrous Ö as sex and violence have flowed from the screen to the street in the form of murders, suicides, rapes, venereal disease, sodomy, divorce, and a wholesale destruction of the family.

The War for Souls

By 1985, when the Christian Film & Television Commission (the "Commission") was started, Hollywood's toxic contamination levels were stratospheric. The Commission launched a two-pronged attack:

Educating moral Americans to become media-wise through MEDIA-WISE FAMILY seminars and through MOVIEGUIDE (800-899-6684, "http://www.movieguide.org" www.movieguide.org) so that they can vote with their cash at the box office as well as write the studio heads to congratulate, castigate, or suggest improvements on their offerings; and

Helping media leaders understand the concerns of moral Americans. By the grace of God, entertainment companies are submitting more scripts to us for review. More and more questions about Christianity and the Christian marketplace are being directed to our offices at the Commission. In fact, we have even been given the opportunity to work on scripts for some of the top television programs and major movies.

The battle lines have been drawn for some time now. The issues become more sharply drawn by the day. The Lord is sending us more and more troops every year, and they have the dedication and talent we so desperately need! We're starting to win many of these battles. A recent example of a major victory:

Many studies have proved that PG-13 ratings attract the 13-and-under crowd. R-ratings are the main things 17-and-under kids want to see. So for years Hollywood, with its eye on a dollar, has been producing sex-and-violence movies designed to pique the curiosity of these vulnerable kids and to make sure they get stamped with the PG-13 and R-ratings which will ensure their box-office success!

Then came the deadly shootings at Columbine High School.

Dr. Baehr helped produce a segment on an entertainment news program on PaxTV which showed that movie theaters were not enforcing the R-rating, which is meant to prevent kids age 17 and under from seeing such movies unless accompanied by a parent or adult guardian.

In the wake of the program, and following pressure from federal government officials emboldened by scientific data provided by MOVIEGUIDE and other groups, many theaters and theater chains across the United States began strictly enforcing the R-rating guidelines.

A study done by the research group, MarketCast, showed that, although many young teens wanted to see R-rated movies, most said they could not get in because of the new enforcement of age restrictions at most movie theaters. The study concluded that "significant numbers" of children under 17, especially girls, were prevented from seeing R-rated movies.

More specifically, this is resulting in current movies such as The Mexican and Angel Eyes losing as much as 40% of potential opening weekend earnings.

The other side understands what is at stake. Feminist, homosexual, abortion, secular humanist, and other groups have banded together to lobby the entertainment media to establish an anti-Christian, anti-human agenda in the entertainment industry. But, as we speak the truth in love, many of our enemies are learning to understand, and even respect us. His love is drawing them into His Kingdom. We take our orders from One Who was known for his friends: IRS types, whores, sinners, and other non-religious folks.

"Christian writers are needed to bring the arts back to the church and to send missionaries to Hollywood," Christian arts advocate Barbara Nicolosi told participants in the fourth annual Christian Writers' Conference at Glorieta. "We have to reach people in Hollywood with our prayers first; then, we can reach them with our witness and our actions." She urges the church to try to study Hollywood's culture instead of just criticizing it. "Missions begin when we go to them and listen. We go, we look and we see how the Spirit of God is preparing the way for the Word. We affirm what is good, we build on it and then we share what we have." Because of the church's constant criticism, Hollywood will "perceive us as brain-numb naysayers. They don't get us. When all they hear us say is 'no,' 'bad,' and 'don't,' they react." Nicolosi urged conference participants to encourage young people to pursue the arts and become missionaries. "Beg them to be writers, artists, poets and film makers," she urged. "If we don't get good Christian kids in the acting profession, we'll never have good Christian role models in Hollywood." This is our Hollywood. This is the mission field to which He has assigned us. The "go ye into all the world" part of the Great Commission clearly includes Hollywood. For more information on the Glorieta Writers' Conference see their website at "http://www.glorieta.com" www.glorieta.com or phone (800) 797-4222.

You might think that our main battles are against pornography, violence, New Age and other anti-God philosophies. We have one that's even bigger: movies that show people solving all their problems and Living Happily Ever After — without Jesus Christ. The subtle, pervasive message of many Hollywood productions is that all you have to do is just meet the right boy or girl, win the lottery, be successful by luck or your own efforts, and you either ride happily off into the sunset or end in tragedy, all by yourself, with no reference to Jesus Christ. It's almost always a subconscious message, but after a lifetime of hearing it, even many Christians start living it. This is one reason why the statistics for born-again Christians on divorce, pornography viewing, etc., vary so little from non-Christians.

TV, music, games, and movies that revolve around occultism, humanism, atheism, pantheism, or nihilism dilute the Christian worldview and lure us — and our children — away from Biblical truth. One of our primary goals is to get our readers and hearers to a point of discernment where they instantly recognize these counterfeit worldviews and are able to decisively counter them with the truth of Jesus Christ.

The Annual MOVIEGUIDE Awards

To counter these false world views, in our reviews we note and compliment every instance we can find of moral behavior, Godly principles, and stories or incidents which dramatize Bible truths.

But, we need more movies like this Ö and one of our highly productive efforts to get them is The Annual MOVIEGUIDE Awards
Gala and Report to the Entertainment Industry.   In 1999, we had
about 75 studio executives and filmmakers come to the Awards
Gala, in 2000 we had about 100, and in 2001 we had 150! Fifteen
of these 150 came from the very top echelon of industry opinion
leaders who have the ultimate authority to approve a multi-million
dollar movie or television project or have the power to get it made
and distributed or broadcast.

Active participants in recent Movieguide Awards events have
included Judith Tukich, the Director of Special Projects for ABC
who gave the go-ahead to broadcast this year's Epiphany Prize win-
ner for Most Inspiring TV Program The Miracle Maker, and William
Fay, who puts together successful movie deals like Independence
Day and The Patriot, two previous Movieguide award winners.
These John Templeton Foundation $25,000 Epiphany awards are a
powerful influence toward Hollywood's appreciation of its
Christian audience. Although this annual gala is an expensive
proposition to put on, the 2001 production was blessed with over
$600,000 in donated services from highly talented people!

Seven major studios control 95% or more of the box office,
plus most of the other mass media of entertainment. With regard
to movies, there are about 30 financial and studio people who can
green light projects, and about 300 key players (executive producers
and a few directors and actors) who can easily get movies made by the
major studios. Every year the Lord gives us more favor and influence
with these people who, for better or for worse, directly or indirectly
affect the character development of our children. We now realize that
our interaction with these key industry leaders does far more good in
bringing about positive change than do attacks or even boycotts.

Is Hollywood Ready for the Good News?   Is it ever!

As we were writing this, a major studio placed an ad in Movieguide. This is another example of how Hollywood really wants the Christian market. Consider the following:

• In 1991, 68 out of 260 movies or 26% had positive moral content. By 2000, this number had shot up to 179 out of 288 or 62%, a 163% increase!

• In 1991, 27 out of 260 movies or 10% had positive spiritual content. By 2000, this number had shot up to 118 out 288 movies or 41%, a 337% increase!

• From 1996 to 2000, the box office earnings of moral movies went from an average of $8.5 million to $48.7 million.

• The average earnings of movies with strong redemptive and/or Christian content went from $2.1 million in 1997 to $18.0 million in 1998, $25.6 million in 1999, and $35.2 million in 2000!

• In 2000, movies with a very strong moral and/or biblical worldview averaged $33.5 million at the box office. By contrast, movies with very strong pagan, occult, politically correct, and secular humanist worldviews averaged $23.6, $10.9, $6.8, and $4.1 million respectively. Movies with very strong immoral, anti-biblical, anti-Semitic, anti-Christian, communist, and radical environmentalist worldviews averaged from $2.2 million on down to $17,000!

"Good guys finish first," Dr. Baehr asserts. "Movies with good Christian content do much better at the box office than others. While everyone else, including the Academy of Motion Picture Arts and Sciences, were hyping movies like The Cider House Rules, Boys

Don't Cry and American Beauty, which averaged less than $26 million at the box office in 1999, decent movies like Toy Story 2, Tarzan and Stuart Little, which critics completely ignored in their Ten Best lists, posted an average of more than $153 million in ticket sales!

People Get It Now!! There is a tremendous Demand for Moral, Christian Entertainment.

You can't say you don't know anymore. God is moving — God style. In other words, in a big way. The July 16, 2001 cover of Newsweek screams, JESUS ROCKS! CHRISTIAN ENTERTAINMENT MAKES A JOYFUL NOISE. The cover story starts, under a magnificent double-page picture of dozens of teenagers praying intently, "The Glorious Rise of Christian Pop. With big best sellers, new movies and religious rock, the $3 billion Christian entertainment industry is exploding."

Using the Christian rock star-studded Festival Con Dios traveling road show with pictures of vibrant, smiling, happy Christian kids as a backdrop, Newsweek quotes 15-year-old Brendan Brown, as he walks through the huge inflatable entrance to the Con Dios main stage, "This is the coolest thing, in my opinion, that has ever happened to Christian music, 180,000 more kids will have taken this walk by the close of the tour on Sept. 30."

With numerous Moms and Dads, and whole families sitting together on blankets in the main-stage area watching ten top-flight bands perform, Newsweek philosophizes: "The values of Christianity and anti-values of rock seem morally incompatible. Yet there's something about the ethos of alternative rock — staying true to your beliefs, never bowing to mainstream pressure — that is oddly simpatico with conservative Christian culture. 'I think rebellion and Christianity go together,' says Mark Stuart, 33, lead singer of Audio Adrenaline, a veteran CCM (Christian Contemporary Music) group. Singing about sex and drugs is old by now. So pretty much the most rebellious rock-and-roll person you can be is a Christian-rock front-man because you get people from every side trying to shut you down.' In another twist, much of the consternation over Christian rock comes from evangelical circles. 'The Christian people protesting our shows call it high-decibel Devil worship,' says Stuart. 'They don't even know what we're doing. They're just afraid. They probably saw Jerry Lee Lewis shaking his hips 50 years ago and are still like "Rock and roll, it's Devil's music." "

This is where we have to move from being defensive to being proactive —and this is where we need and would welcome your help:

a. Show your church how to benefit from the good stuff and punish the bad stuff Hollywood puts out by referring to "http://www.movieguide.org" www.movieguide.org and other material available from that website.

b.Let us know about any successful take-it-to-the-world productions your church is doing. We can use your example for other churches to emulate and be encouraged.

You can help us recruit an army of Christian scriptwriters, producers, financiers (Yes! There's very good box office money for high-end Christian productions), directors, actors, and supporting personnel whom God has enabled and talented, to eradicate the anemic filth our opposition (with rapidly decreasing success) is still trying to make money on. Remember, we're not trying to eradicate them, but to win them to Jesus so they become successful and productive in turning out good stuff for the glory of God! This has happened so many times already, and to the worst of the worst, that we're expecting it to keep on happening more and more! We're rejoicing! We're winning!

Maybe your church already has an active audiotape/videotape library. The following idea might help you start or improve its services by adding proactive teaching to parents and kids on how to view movies and TV programs:

Some Sunday during announcements, ask for a show of hands of families who own more than, say, five Christian videos. Ask them to meet briefly with yourself or a pre-designated person (have that person stand as you introduce them, in the place he or she will meet them) after the service, to discuss the possibility of putting together your video library. If one or more of these people agree to taking on this ministry, give them a copy of The Media-Wise Family by Dr. Ted Baehr, and, in a private meeting, go over with them how they can have a real ministry teaching parents and kids dozens of ways to enliven their TV and video viewing by looking at everything the way God looks at it.

Then, encourage the use of MOVIEGUIDE so your church families will be able to know, ahead of time, what they're getting into when they rent a video or go to a movie. Indeed, your church could have an excellent video library that people could borrow movies from. Why allow the temptation of the local video store?

Online churches - the wave of the future?

David Yonggi Cho, pastor of the 750,000-member Yoido Full Gospel Church in Seoul, South Korea, and Rick Warren, pastor of the 15,000-member Saddleback Valley Community Church met recently in California to discuss church growth strategies for the 21st century, and their conclusion was — stop building buildings and use that money for world missions. (From the July 25, 2001 issue of Rick Warren's Ministry Toolbox, a free, e-mail newsletter available from the website"http://www.pastors.com" www.pas-

tors.com as quoted in "http://www.joelnews.org"
www.joelnews.org)

With 20,000 new converts a year, Cho says there is no way his church can match buildings to membership, so he's encouraging younger converts to stay at home and worship through the Internet. These long-distance members give regular feedback on the sermons and services, they can give their tithe through the Internet, and they stay physically connected to the larger body through small study groups. "It is silly to build larger and larger church buildings. It is silly to spend more money on branch church buildings. You'll never have enough," Cho says.

Rick Warren, the author of The Purpose Driven Church adds," Our goal is to centralize — to send our church members out for ministry into their neighborhoods." Regarding the traditional need for buildings, Warren cites Saddleback's legacy: "We wanted to prove to the world that you don't have to have a building to grow a church. We were running over 10,000 in attendance before we built our first building." (They met in a high school.)

Cho says this strategy does not mean you completely abandon a central church building. He says, "We need both ministries together — a strong, young church and a very powerful Internet service." He says this helps the local church to minister worldwide. "There are many American-Koreans participating in our church's ministry through the Internet," says Cho. "Through the Internet, we can have worldwide fellowship and worldwide services."

A Barna Research Group study shows the Internet is one of the fastest developing areas in the ministry world today. More than 100,000 Protestant churches already minister to people through the Web, the study found. According to Barna, within this decade as many as 50 million individuals may rely solely upon the

Internet to provide all of their faith-based experiences. "We foresee two-thirds of people engaging in Net-based religious pursuits on a regular basis as the decade progresses, such as listening to archived religious teaching, reading online devotionals, and buying religious products and resources online."

The Barna study shows virtually every dimension of the faith community will be influenced by online faith developments through the likes of self-produced and self-marketed worship music, e-mail broadcasting, theological chats, online meetings, broadcasts to congregants who are immobile, live webcasting of mission trips, and 24/7 ministry training from the best trainers and educators in the world!

In 1999, Yonggi Cho was invited to preach in Dubai. During the services, the authorities came to tell him, "If you ever move [your meetings] out of the British Embassy, you will be arrested." Yet, about 3,000 Islamic young people kept coming to Cho's services. Cho asked them how they even knew there were services, since the police were trying to squelch the meetings. They said, "Through your Internet services! In Saudi Arabia, we have no church, and we can't own a Bible, but we can still read the Internet. We are watching your Internet service and you announced that you were coming to Dubai — so we took our vacations and came out [of Saudi.]"

Saudi Arabia is the most closed country in the world to the Good News of Jesus Christ. Expatriates caught in worship services are jailed and/or deported. Saudis who become Christians are routinely killed. The same is true in many other Moslem countries. Are your internet outreaches designed to interest, convert, and disciple the English-speaking children of Libya, Saudi Arabia, Turkmenistan, India, and China? (China is said to have more people who understand English than any other country in the world.)

A Kingdom Goal!

Following are a few examples of ministry others have done, plus a few far-out ideas. We challenge you before God to see if your church, your ministry, could be used by God to do something even greater, for the glory of Jesus Christ. You "get it," now get cool. Do it — in a big way.

In California, in some of the art communities, Christian artists and their churches hold art shows that attract a great public audience for art, music, food, and fun. These artists get to do what they love best and then they quietly, and sometimes not so quietly, spread the word of God. Someone always asks, "What's that little note in the corner of the painting, Jn 3:16?" Why are these paintings so beautiful? There's nothing dark about them. They celebrate life!

A wonderful and big church in Malibu, California does not have a sanctuary to worship God. It has a "Performing Arts Center." That's the sanctuary. And why not? God created the arts, music, books, writing, etc. That church has a God idea. God is taking back His territory in the arts. Stages everywhere are becoming Holy Ground! That's cool. That's God in action.

Recently in the small town of Huntsville, Arkansas, 125 young people gave their lives to Jesus as a result of four performances of Heaven's Gates and Hell's Flames in First Baptist. Based on Rev. 20:12-15, this highly successful drama, which grippingly portrays the judgment of this terrible separation from God as well as the wonders of waking up in heaven to live and reign with Christ forever, has been producing similar fruit for years. A highly dedicated three-person ministry team quickly coaches local and even first-time actors into a first-rate performance.

See"http://www.mze.com/heavensgates/" www.mze.com/heavens-gates/

The Bema, by Tim Stevenson, is another life-changing high drama. All the production requires is a narrator, an 18-foot-high angel, a heavenly choir (yours will do) and a few simple sound effects. It makes a highly effective sermon replacement if continued over two Sundays. We heard a tape of a superb dramatization by Pete Briscoe, Senior Pastor, Bent Tree Bible Fellowship in Carrollton, Texas. Available in any bookstore, The Bema is the story of a day in the life of one very marginal Christian by the name of Daniel Mathewson. It starts out like any other day, but turns out to be The Day! The Lord comes, and suddenly Mathewson is in Glory watching the intense drama of the Bema Judgment unfold as saint after saint down through the ages goes before the Lord to watch his life's work pass through the judgment fires and receive his rewards for what survives. Tension builds as it gets close to the time for the Lord to review his life. If you want your people to live for The Day instead of today, this Scripture-based drama will change the lives of more than a few.

In 1994 a church in Spartanburg, South Carolina expected 150 kids to sign up for a basketball program which stresses evangelism, character building, and learning basic basketball. 450 signed up, and "Upward Basketball" was off and running. This past year, over 100,000 children along with many of their parents were participating nationwide. See "http://www.upward.org" www.upward.org or call 800-585-4721.

Imagine stories so powerful that without even a PA system or stage, all kinds of people will go way out to the wilderness on the far side of their Jordans to hear them. Imagine spirit-inspired music so powerful that a band, or even a single musician, could start performing it on any street or mall in the world, and soon crowds of thousands would gather to hear the Message.

Imagine talent with the boldness, imagination, and vision to walk into the unreached tribes of the world with nothing but a video camera and a script (worked out with one of the many talented people God has already sent us from every country in the world)... boldly taking charge for Jesus and quickly doing the casting, getting them to memorize the lines, building the enthusiasm, and within days or even hours producing a rough but effective Good News story in video which could immediately be taken to the next village, to ask if they could do it any better ... then coming back a while later to do the next Good News story, and the next, and to plant a church there which already knows how to go out and not only plant other churches, but to plant them into other people groups, even (because of what God has done in them) among their enemies.

All over the unreached parts of the world, billions of people are waiting for God's story-tellers, bards, Shakespeares, and musicians to bring them the Message, God's great Good News stories, in their language.

Could God use you to inspire your church to take its ministry to the streets, to Hollywood, to the ends of the earth? Yes! Go! Go! Go! Get out of your buildings. Go spread the Word to the four corners of the Earth.

CHAPTER SEVEN

THE PASTOR'S BUSINESS

Curtis W. Wallace

Minimizing Risk and Maximizing Potential

Over the last half-century, the dynamics of the church have changed dramatically. Progress in the fields of radio, television, publishing, the internet, and entertainment have made it possible for a local pastor to reach an audience of incredible size and scope. The seating capacity of the sanctuary no longer dictates the reach of the message. Today, a preacher standing alone in a television studio can reach an audience far larger than the crowd addressed by the preacher standing before tens of thousands in a football stadium. Moreover, some great men of God are combining the elements of a huge stadium event with electronic distribution through television, via satellite, the internet, and radio to reach most of the world's population. In this environment, it is no surprise that many of today's leading ministers are starting to compete with Hollywood's elite in terms of the audience that they reach.

In fact, recent statistics show that over 170 million Americans attend some type of church service on a weekly basis. This is an audience, in terms of its size, that Hollywood only dreams about. By comparison, the total movie going audience for a given week is only 15 to 25 million people (depending how big the movie is for that week). That means that church reaches an audience that is 7 to 10 times the size of the audience that the movie studios reach each week.

More and more, ministries are using the tools of media conglomerates to more effectively reach and communicate with the vast audience of church-goers in this country. Effective use of the available media in turn leads to a level of exposure that causes the secular media to take notice. In a time when every significant player in corporate America is driven to reach as many eyeballs as possible, everyone from movie producers, to record companies, to publishers, to banks are starting to see the wisdom of reaching the vast audience that the church represents.

Moreover, advances in technology and distribution are making it possible for smaller and smaller ministries to begin the process of reaching out to the masses. For example, it is now possible for a small church to broadcast its services over the internet for only a few hundred dollars per week. This means that ministers must be prepared to deal with the realities of the entertainment economy.

In today's world a myriad of entertainment related opportunities are available. In many cases, these opportunities are best dealt with outside of the corporate structure of the church or ministry. That being the case, this chapter, along with Tom Gehring's chapter on taking your ministry to Hollywood, will try to assist in not only evaluating the opportunities that are presented to you, but also in structuring your personal business in a way that allows you to maximize your opportunities.

Why form your own business

When presented with a new business opportunity, the initial

inclination of many pastors is to conduct personal business through their existing non-profit ministry. Many pastors think, for example, that the non-profit status of the ministry will aid in reducing taxes or enable them to use church staff on the project.

However, these reasons need to be examined. First, you need to remember what a non-profit corporation is and is not. A non-profit corporation is not owned by anyone. In reality, a non-profit corporation is owned by the public at large and the state has the right to insure that its assets are only used for non-profit purposes. On the other hand, a for-profit company is owned by its shareholders. That means that the shareholders can do what they wish with the company and its assets. In addition, no limits exist on the amount of money a minister can earn from his or her own company. As you know, the "excess benefit" and private inurement laws effectively limit the income that you can earn from your ministry.

Lets look at an example. Pastor Johnson heads a large, growing church. In addition, he is starting to get requests to speak at conferences, conventions, and churches and has drawn the attention of a major book publisher. If Pastor Johnson contracts with the publisher through the church instead of his own company, the following will be the result:

The ministry will receive the royalties and will not pay tax on the amount that it receives. Any money paid to Pastor Johnson by the church is compensation and triggers two things. First, all of the money paid to Pastor Johnson is income to him and is taxed at ordinary income rates. Second, the payments to Pastor Johnson are part of his total compensation from the ministry and must meet requirements of reasonableness. This may not be an issue now, but if Pastor Johnson's ministry grows and the book succeeds and earns significant royalty income, Pastor Johnson may not even be able to receive the blessing conveyed through the book because he gets to the point where his church salary maxes out.

The ministry will now own the copyright to the book, a very valuable asset. This means that Pastor Johnson's children cannot inherit the copyright. At some point, a transaction would have to take place to transfer that copyright to Pastor Johnson and his family. Moreover, consideration must be paid for that transfer and that consideration must be fair. Worse, if Pastor Johnson, for some reason leaves his church, he will not own the copyright.

The results are easy to judge. Pastor Johnson will still pay taxes, assuming that the church can legitimately pay him the money at all, will not own a valuable asset and as a result, that asset cannot be a legacy to his family unless he buys it back at some point.

On the other hand, if Pastor Johnson had created Pastor Johnson Incorporated, the result would be much more beneficial. All of the royalties would be paid to Pastor Johnson, without question as to amount or reasonableness. The income would be taxable, just as if it were paid from the church. However, owning your own company will open options for tax and estate planning that can provide benefits as well. In addition, the copyright can be controlled and freely transferred to others. Pastor Johnson now has a valuable asset to leave to his family and create a legacy.

Personal business opportunities open up not only the potential for increased, unrestricted income, and creating a legacy for your family, but just as importantly, open up venues for your creative efforts. By their nature, most ministers are creative people. Be it writing and delivering a sermon or writing and singing a song, ministry is inherently creative. Most creative people need multiple outlets through which they can breath life into their creative thoughts and inspirations.

Very often, some of your best investments may be investing into your own creative thoughts. Even a minister with limited financial resources can invest his or her time to create a new product such as a book, a song, a play, or some other concept. Once that vision becomes real, numerous opportunities exist for exploitation of the creation.

Points of Concern

Clearly, ample reasons exist for many ministers to form their own business entities. Therefore, the discussion moves to how a business should be set-up and structured to maximize opportunities and minimize risk.

The primary liability concern is avoiding IRS entanglement. The IRS has two principal concerns with regard to your business: (1) whether your company properly reports income and pays its taxes (the same concern it has with every person and business), and (2) whether the dealing between your company and your ministry are fair and reasonable. The first concern is common to everyone and will not be addressed here except to say that you should find a competent CPA to help you with tax and financial planning.

On the second issue, all of the IRS rules with regard to private inurement and excess benefits apply to dealings between your ministry and your business. This means (1) you cannot use ministry assets without paying for them, and (2) any deals between your business and your ministry must be fair and reasonable.

Continuing the example with Pastor Johnson, consider two points. First, if Pastor Johnson uses his church secretary to type the transcript of his book, the church must be compensated for the use of her services or the service must be valued and added to Pastor Johnson's compensation. Why is this necessary? The church secretary is paid by the church and therefore, her time during regular church office hours belongs to the ministry and cannot be used for private activities unless the church is compensated. Therefore, Pastor Johnson should hire someone outside of the ministry or make sure that the church is properly compensated.

This issue of separateness can be very problematic in practice. Therefore, if the Pastor's business is significant enough to justify it, the pastor should set-up a totally separate office with a separate staff, separate credit arrangements and accounts. Until you reach this point, you will simply need to be careful to maintain separateness between ministry and personal activities.

On a related point, make sure that your travel arrangements are properly handled. If you personally receive honoraria, you need to personally pay the cost of travel to the engagement (or have the hosting ministry pay the cost).

The next issue is fairness of those transactions that do take place between your business and your ministry. Such transactions are common for ministers who are engaged in music or writing. Most publishing contracts allow the author to purchase copies of the work from the publisher at deeply discounted prices (60%-80% off of retail) and resell those copies in specified (usually non-retail) sales channels. Given this ability, it is often very attractive for all parties concerned for the minister to resell copies of the book to the ministry for resale. Such an arrangement is perfectly fine, as long as the deal is fair. In this case, the ministry should get as good of a deal or better than it can get otherwise. If the ministry can buy from a distributor at a 45% discount, it cannot buy from the minister at a 40% discount. It needs to buy at a 45% or better discount. To be safe, make sure that the ministry gets a better deal than it would get directly from the distributors.

In summary, if the deal is fair and separateness is maintained, it is unlikely that your business or ministry will be in jeopardy from the IRS.

Have an Employment Agreement

In order to comply with the foregoing, it is very important for all ministers to have an employment agreement. An employment agreement between you and your ministry will help to define who owns what, what is included in your approved compensation package.

For example, under copyright law, the creative works of an employee are generally the property of the employer, unless there is an agreement to the contrary. Thus, absent an agreement to the contrary, the text of your Sunday messages may be owned by the Church. Similarly, a music minister's songs may be the property of the church in the absence of a contrary agreement. Accordingly, the existence of a well thought out employment agreement can avoid later problems.

Such an agreement needs to be put in place at the outset of a ministry, if at all possible. This will avoid later changes that dramatically alter the nature of the employment relationship. Among the factors that should be included in an employment agreement are:

Salary

Job Description — specify exactly what the pastor must do to earn the salary

Clarify intellectual property rights — at a minimum all of the pastor's outside creative endeavors (such as book and music writing) should be his own property. In addition, he or she should have the right to derive materials from his sermons and teaching that were prepared for delivery at the church

Clearly state what church assets (cars, planes, etc) the pastor has the right to use and the value of those services

The length of the agreement

In addition to the concerns set forth above, a few additional points should be considered. First, you need to know that your own for-profit company will not be able to avail itself of the many constitutional protections that are available to the church. This means that all of the laws and regulations that apply to any other business will apply to yours.

The most significant point of concern is religious discrimination. As you probably know, a church can discriminate in hiring on the basis of its honestly held religious beliefs. This means that a church that chooses to do so, can freely terminate an individual whose conduct or religious beliefs violate those of the church. Unlike most companies, a church can properly ask its employees about their religious beliefs and affiliations and ask those employees to conform to a code of conduct that has its basis in the church's religious beliefs.

Your for-profit corporation cannot do this. You cannot even ask questions about religious issues in the course of an interview. You will need to be very careful in how you go about identifying employees. In addition, you can and should make very clear to applicants what is expected in the job. For instance that an employee will need to be comfortable interacting and conducting business within the Christian community.

Evaluating Opportunities

As you move into the business world, carefully consider your opportunities. Some of the best advice I can give you is to do what you do. What I mean is simply this, business ventures that take advantage of your unique gifts are far more likely to be successful than business ventures that do not. When you look at a venture, carefully consider what you bring to the table on the deal. This will tell you if you are just an investor or if you have a special position within the deal.

As a pastor, you are likely to be approached with business offers that stretch across the spectrum from real estate to backing inventions. In my position as Chief Operating Officer of T.D. Jakes Enterprises, Inc., I have been amazed by the proposals that have come across my desk. The proposals come from every possible direction, from Fortune 500 Companies to Sister Susie who bakes cookies. Whether you want to or not, you are going to need to develop a system for responding to inquiries.

When you are approached with new deals every day, like we are at T.D. Jakes Enterprises, you have to be able to quickly and effectively separate the real deals from the dogs. A big part of my job is to evaluate potential offers and bring forward those deals that make sense and have significant potential. If I waste Bishop Jakes' time with deals that do not make sense, I wouldn't be here for long. To accomplish my objective and quickly evaluate whether a proposal has merit, I look at the following points:

Consider the Source — Did this proposal or idea come from a reliable and competent source? Did the deal come to you through someone that you know, trust, and respect? There are a number of people that I have tremendous respect for within the Christian business community. That respect has been earned over years of experience. If one of the people that I respect brings something to my attention, I will take time to carefully evaluate the offer. I may say no, but not before I check it out.

Likewise, certain people can send me a proposal and I will just smile while I am putting it in the trash. Time is too precious to waste. If the last two things that you brought me were garbage, chances are awfully good that I am not going to spend time on your next deal.

If I do not know you, the source that referred you becomes important. If you impressed someone who I know is credible, that gives you credibility with me. I will listen to a proposal because I know that you have already passed one pretty good filter.

This brings up a good related point. Sometimes people will refer a person to someone else, not because they thought the deal was good, but because they wanted to get the person out of their office. While this may be expedient, it can lower your credibility rating because now you are wasting my time with a deal you knew was bad. Just be honest. Tell the man his deal is no good and move on. Don't harm your own credibility by wasting an associate's time.

Choose Long-Term Partners. Real success is rarely achieved the first time that you do something. Significant results are built over time. This means that you need partners who are in business for the long-term. Long-term partners must have integrity and the ability to work with others over time. Short-term partners inevitably miss the big rewards because they are after the quick buck.

Finding such partners is easier said than done. But it is critically important. The integrity, commitment, and knowledge of your partners is often more important to your long-term success than the quality of the deal. For example, you can get the greatest book deal in the world, with a big advance and great royalty rate, but if your publisher decides not to aggressively market your book, your long-term value as an author will be diminished because you (not the publisher) will be labeled as an author who does not sell.

One of three things will happen when you enter into a business relationship — it will either go great, it will go bad, or it will do just OK. In two of those circumstances, integrity is key. If the deal goes good, some people get greedy and think that they should get more than the contract says. When it goes bad, people try to avoid a loss and when they do that, they start fighting.

When you are evaluating a deal, this can be difficult to judge. However, your instincts will help you. If a potential partner keeps trying to move the deal around before you ever have a deal, he will probably try to do the same after you have a deal. In the few cases where I have had to fight to get a deal, I have usually regretted it deal after it was over. I do not mean that deals should not be negotiated. I have had some very tough negotiations with people who I respect and will always do business with. That is the way the world should work. What I am talking about is the potential partner who is very clearly trying to take advantage and has that scent of sleaze that permeates all that they do.

Carefully checking out potential business partners will also save you a lot of headaches. If someone stinks up enough offices, it usually cannot by hidden for long. By making calls to people that they have done business with (I mean people you find — not the ones they refer you too), you can get the real skinny pretty quickly. The bottom-line is whether you can see yourself in a long-term business relationship with the person. Individual business transactions are rarely as profitable as long-term relationships and you are not going to have long-term relationships with short-term people.

Does It Fit Your Mission?

This is a key filter for deals that pass Number 1 and Number 2. You need to know what you are trying accomplish with your business. Once you know where you are going, you can judge whether a potential deal fits within your vision for your company. If you need to adjust your vision to fit the deal, you probably should pass on the deal. More simply put, do what you do.

Does it fit on a napkin?

Good business arrangements should make sense. If a deal involves elements that you do not understand, there may be a problem. I am not talking about all of the legalese in a 50-page contract — that is what lawyers are for. I am talking about the basic elements of the business arrangements. You should be able to reduce the deal to a picture on a napkin. Every deal should come down to "I will do this, you will do that, I get this and you get that." How you get there may be complicated, but the essence needs to be that simple.

Can you afford a fight with this partner?

Be very careful about entering into business relationships with people who you cannot get into a fight with. We all want to maintain harmonious business relationships. That, however, is not always possible. Sometimes people just do the wrong thing. When that happens you will try to resolve the problem. But, if you can't resolve the problem, you will have to choose. You will either fight or you will take the abuse. If you do business with someone who, for some reason, you cannot or should not fight with, you lose options. When you lose options, the other party gains leverage.

This means that you need to be careful about doing business with family, prominent church members, and anyone else who may be in a position to detrimentally impact your life separate and apart from the deal.

If the deal looks good and passes the 5 tests, you may have something. At this point you should seek a Multitude of Counsel. Ask people that you trust what they think. Talk to people with varied perspectives and backgrounds and get input. Someone else may have that critical piece of information that helps you make the best possible deal.

Negotiating a Deal

At this point, I want to talk about some of the points to think about in negotiating a deal. Since there is an endless variety of deals that you may enter into, I am going to discuss important elements related to the two most common business transactions for pastors — the book deal and music deal.

Money

In any deal, the big issue is money. In the book and music businesses, money typically comes in three forms. The first is the advance (if you have some negotiating power). Most book publishers and record companies will pay an advance against future royalties. The negotiation points are straightforward. The artist wants the largest advance possible and the company wants to pay the smallest advance possible. It is a matter of risk avoidance on both sides of the fence. The artist wants to know he or she is getting paid (without having to wade through publisher or record company accounting to get there) and more importantly, that the company is committed to the project. When a record company or publisher puts out significant up-front money, that company tends to be motivated to earn its money back. From its standpoint, the publisher/record company doesn't mind paying the money — they just don't want to pay it until they have sales to justify the money. In a perfect world, the advance paid would be a little less than the total royalties earned by the artist/author on the project. In such a case, neither side took an unreasonable risk.

One important note, an up-front payment from a publisher or record company is called an advance because it is recoupable out of royalties. This means that the company will retain all of your earned royalties until such time as they have been repaid the entire amount advanced.

With regard to royalties, important differences exist in the book world between the Christian and secular markets and between the book and record worlds. In the book world, Christian and secular publishers use two different standards. For the most part, Christian publishers pay royalties as a percentage of the publisher's sales. This means that the publisher pays you a percentage of the wholesale price of the book. Typically, royalties range from 10% — 30%, depending on the strength of the author.

Here is how is works in practice:

Number of books sold 200,000 units

Retail price $20.00

Wholesale Price $10.00 (a 50% discount is common)

Total Publisher Sales $2,000,000.00

Royalty Rate 20%

Royalty Earned $400,000.00

If the book does not sell, the publisher will simply drop the wholesale price (which allows the retailer to discount the price) and the author is paid on the actual sale price of the items. In addition, the publisher will have deductions, returns, and free goods.

On the other hand, secular publishers use a much more complicated system based on the retail price of the item. A scale is used for discounts in the retail price of the item. Because of the retail price basis used to calculate the royalty, secular publishers pay lower royalty rates (all other factors being equal). Generally, 12% — 15% is common among the secular publishers dealing with established authors.

In theory, here is how it works for a secular publisher:

Number of books sold 200,000 units

Retail price $20.00

Wholesale Price not applicable

Total Retail Sales $4,000,000.00

Royalty Rate 15%

Royalty Earned $600,000.00

The reality is much more complicated for secular publishers. Their accounting systems and contracts approach those of the movie studios in terms of complexity. The result is that the real game with secular publishers is the advance. You should never count on recouping your advance. The advance is what the negotiation is all about. Christian publishers, on the other hand, generally lack the financial capacity to fund large advances and as a result, the negotiation is all about the royalty rate.

With music, because the five major record companies directly or indirectly have control over most of the significant Christian music labels, the two-tiered system that exists for books does not exist for music. The royalty system is somewhat similar to the system used by secular book publishers — it is based on the retail price of the product and is similarly complicated.

The important distinction is that the artist pays for virtually everything. In a typical artist music contract, not only is the advance recoupable out of the artist's royalties, but the cost of production is also recoupable. In addition, the royalties that are paid to the producers of the project are paid out of the artist's royalties.

Here is how this works:

Artist Advance	$50,000
Production Expenses	$150,000
Artist Royalty Rate	12%
Producer's Royalty Rate	3%
Artists True Royalty Rate	9%
Units Sold	100,000
Retail Price	$15.00
Total Sales$	1,500,000.00
Royalties Earned	$135,000.00
Less Advances Paid	($200,000.00)
Royalty Owed	nothing

This example also fails to reflect a variety of items such as packaging discounts and other partially or fully recoupable expenses such as music video production, tour support, and the cost of outside marketing firms.

The simple result of this illustration is that music deals typically center on a negotiation of the advance. Because of the record company's ability to recoup its expenses, the advance is the most tangible element of the deal.

This also illustrates another important point in dealing with record labels, you are as responsible as they are for watching the budget. If you go way over budget, the record label may pay the bills right now, but you will pay them back out of the royalties.

In addition to advances and royalties, artists and authors have the opportunity to earn significant sums through their own sales of the products. Generally, publishers and record companies allow artists to purchase copies of the product at a significant discount off of the retail price (generally 50% — 80% off). The artist/author is then free to resell the items at events and appearances, but typically not through any retail sales channels (you can't sell copies to the local bookstore). A pastor speaking at a large number of events can generate significant income in this manner.

Length of the Deal

The length of a book or record contract is critical point for both parties. From the artist/author standpoint, you want to free to renegotiate a new better deal if the book or record is successful. Likewise, the publisher/record company wants to be able to benefit from its significant investment in marketing your name. Particularly in the record business, it often takes 3-4 albums and marketing campaigns to build an audience and position an artist for a break-out project. As a result, the record company does not want to be in the position of spending years of time and hundreds of thousands of dollars only to see the hit record come with a competing label. As with advances, a balance is usually struck in a well negotiate deal. From the standpoint of books, shorter terms are generally acceptable with deals for 2-3 books being common. In the music business, a 4-6 record deal is more the norm.

Marketing Support.

While it is fairly rare in either book or music deals for the company to guarantee a certain level of marketing support. However, this point should be well discussed and if possible, included in the deal. A project that lacks support will not succeed. A key element in whether your project will have proper marketing support is whether the PEOPLE in the company support you and your project. Never forget that businesses are run by people. It takes a person to stick his neck out and ask for a certain budget to get a job done. You need to be sure that the people you do business with are ready to stand behind you and your project. This also means that you need to know and have support from highly placed executives in that company. It does you no good if the people supporting you have no power.

Rights Granted

Make sure that you clearly understand what rights you are not giving to the company. For instance, a book contract that is not negotiated will grant a publisher television and film rights to your book, as well as the right to do abridgements and compilations. Your story could end up in a movie and you have nothing to say about it. In addition, the publisher will end up with part of the price paid by the movie studio for the rights.

Creative Control

Creative control of the project is the last major point. Is the publisher free to edit matters of substance or simply edit for grammar. Can they suggest changes or force changes. Remember, this is a God thing. The publisher wants to sell books. You have a message. Protect the message.

Hopefully the thoughts presented here will aid you in your business endeavors. Many of the concepts discussed with regard to books and music apply to other entertainment industries.

Finally, it is our hope that through the teachings in this book, you have gained valuable knowledge and that our counsel will help you design the very best legal strategies for your 21st Century Church.

About the Authors

CURTIS W. WALLACE

Curtis W. Wallace is a lawyer and the Chief Operating Officer of T. D. Jakes Enterprises, Inc., Touchdown Concepts, Inc. and Dexterity Unlimited, Inc. Prior to joining T. D. Jakes in 1999, he was a corporate and real estate attorney representing businesses, banks and ministries across the country. Mr. Wallace is a Magna Cum Laude graduate of Southern Methodist University School of Law, and holds a Bachelor of Business Administration from the University of Texas, Austin.

BREWER, BREWER, ANTHONY & MIDDLEBROOK

Brewer, Brewer, Anthony & Middlebrook began over four decades ago in Dallas County, Texas. Dennis G. Brewer, Sr. started his law practice in 1954 and in 1980 he was joined by Dennis G. Brewer, Jr. Today, they are a full service law firm located in the Las Colinas area of the Dallas/Ft. Worth Metroplex. They provide legal representation and services to their clients in the following areas:

LITIGATION

Their attorneys practice trial and appellate law in state and federal courts throughout the United States.

CORPORATIONS

They provide a wide range of services to their corporate clients regarding corporate structure and governance issues, real estate transactions, banking and general corporate law, church and First Amendment Law.

INDIVIDUALS

The firm represents individuals and families in family law, personal injury, criminal law and probate and estate matters.

Brewer, Brewer, Anthony & Middlebrook is a law firm of dedicated attorneys and staff who are devoted to one important goalóa complete commitment to their clients and their success. They have a long tradition of winning trial lawyers. The firm is actively engaged in all areas of trial and appellate practice including:

CIVIL LITIGATION

The firm represents both plaintiffs and defendants in all types of civil matters including business disputes, insurance claims, real estate transactions, employment litigation and banking transactions.

FAMILY LAW

Their family law attorneys represent individuals and families involved in divorce, modification and enforcement, paternity and adoption matters. In addition, they counsel clients on pre-marital and post-marital property issues.

TORT LITIGATION

Their clients include individuals who have been significantly injured as a result of negligence, harmful products and malpractice as well as intentional acts.

Brewer, Brewer, Anthony & Middlebrook counsels clients in a variety of business, corporate and transactional matters including:

GENERAL CORPORATE LAW

They handle the creation and structuring of new and existing business entities, including corporations, limited partnerships and limited liability companies.

NON-PROFIT ORGANIZATIONS

The firm has an extensive practice that focuses on non-profit and tax exempt organizations. They represent numerous churches, parachurch ministries, and ministers across the United States.

BUSINESS/REAL ESTATE TRANSACTIONS

The firm represents clients in all areas of business transactions, including the acquisition, financing and disposition of businesses and real estate.

BANKING LAW

Their attorneys provide legal services to lending institutions regarding personal and commercial lending, foreclosures, collections and Small Business Administration loans.

DAVID O. MIDDLEBROOK

David O. Middlebrook is a shareholder in the law firm of Brewer, Brewer, Anthony & Middlebrook, P.C. located in Irving, TX and is the head of the Non-Profit Law Group. His practice includes advising clients on legal questions relating to general corporate and business matters with a special emphasis on legal issues affecting non-profit and faith-based organizations operating in the United States, Canada, United Kingdom, Mexico, India and the Philippines. The Non-Profit Law Group provides counsel to clients in corporate matters, conducts legal compliance reviews, designs and implements employment practices, policies and procedures and advises clients regarding employee benefit and termination issues, compliance under the EEOC, ADA, FMLA, Title VII, and various other federal and state statutes.

Mr. Middlebrook graduated with honors with a B.S. in Business Management in 1985 from Oral Roberts University and earned his Juris Doctor in 1989 from Southern Methodist University. Mr. Middlebrook is a member of the bar in Texas, Colorado, the District of Columbia, the United States Court of Appeals for the Fifth Circuit, and the Federal District Court of the Northern District of Texas. Additionally, he is a member of the American Bar Association, National Employment Lawyers Association, Dallas County Employment Lawyers Association, and is a past President of the Irving Bar Association. Mr. Middlebrook is certified by the Cambridge Program in Risk Management for Churches and Schools offered by the University of Cambridge in Cambridge, England.

Mr. Middlebrook is a frequent guest lecturer at programs and seminars dedicated to practitioners and tax-exempt organizations.

He has authored numerous articles on non-profit topics published in Church Business Magazine and Ministries Today. Mr. Middlebrook is also the author of The Guardian System, a comprehensive system for the prevention of child abuse within an organization, for which he was awarded a 2001 Evangelical Christian Publishers Association Gold Medallion book award in recognition of excellence in evangelical Christian literature.

THOMAS G. GEHRING

Thomas G. Gehring graduated from Pepperdine University School of Law, located in Malibu, California in May 1979 where he received his Juris Doctorate degree. He was a member of the Law Review and was a published author in the law school's Law Review.

Mr. Gehring has his own law practice in West Los Angeles, California, where he specializes in corporate and entertainment law. With 22 years of experience, he has represented and continues to represent many excellent and well-established corporations, production companies, actors and actresses, and filmmakers. He is active with The Christian Film and Television Commission, and many National Ministries involved in the entertainment industry.

Mr. Gehring is an adjunct professor of law at Pepperdine University School of Law and is a sought after speaker on many corporate and entertainment law issues.

Mr. Gehring was born in Baltimore, Maryland. Special interests include writing, rock climbing, playing the piano, and hiking with his cat, Charlie.

WINTERS, KING & ASSOCIATES

WINTERS, KING & ASSOCIATES is a Christian law firm dedicated to meeting the legal needs of people since its inception in
1983. Partners Thomas Winters and Michael King joined together
to create a law practice founded upon the principle that "Lawyers
Can Be Healers"...words engraved upon the doorway of their law
school and alma mater, Oral Roberts University. Together, Tom
Winters and Mike King have carefully selected a trained and experienced staff of six additional attorneys and eleven support personnel who are committed to providing the best legal services possible, from the simplest to the most complex individual and business legal matters. The varied legal backgrounds, range from a
Harvard Law School graduate to a nationally known estate planning expert, but the firm is best known as a leader in representing
Christian churches and organizations. The vast experience and
expertise of these attorneys combined with their Christian commitment serves the clientele of Winters, King & Associates exceptional-
ly well.

Winters, King & Associates specializes in all areas of the law
including non-profit church and ministry law, corporate and business matters, tax exempt law, employment law, estate planning,
wills and trusts, probate, personal injury matters, family and
domestic matters, adoption/guardianships, worker's compensation,
trademark/copyrights, and bankruptcy as well as all phases of litigation by experienced, successful trial attorneys.

The firm has memberships in the state Bar Association, the
American Bar Association, the American Trial Lawyers Association,
Christian Legal Society, Inns of Court, and is licensed to practice
before State, Federal, and U.S. Tax Courts. The partners also serve

on the boards of, and in an advisory capacity to many churches and ministries throughout the United States.

Winters, King & Associates, Inc.

Phone: (918) 494-6868

Facsimile: (918) 491-6297

Email address: twinters@wintersking.com

Mailing address: 2448 E. 81st Street, Suite 5900

Tulsa, Oklahoma, 74137-4259

Thomas J. Winters is the founding partner of the law firm of Winters, King & Associates, Inc. Mr. Winters received his B. A. and J. D. from Oral Roberts University (ORU). He has served as an adjunct professor, teaching church law at the ORU Seminary, and presently teaches as an adjunct professor at Rhema Bible Training Center. He has represented over 3,500 churches, ministries, and other non-profit organizations located throughout the United States and in more than 38 foreign countries.

Mr. Winters' clientele include some of today's best-known national and international ministers and non profit organizations, as well as thousands of smaller organizations. He is licensed to practice law before State, Federal, and U. S. Tax courts.

Mr. Winters also serves as literary agent on behalf of many of today's most popular authors. He has procured significant contracts on behalf of clients with such notable publishers as HarperCollins, Time Warner/AOL, Pengiun Putnam, Thomas Nelson, Word, Harrison House and many others.

Mr. Winters lives in Tulsa, Oklahoma, with his wife, Michelle and their four children.

Dan Beirute joined Winters, King & Associates in 1997 after graduating from Harvard Law School. Dan specializes in representation of churches and ministries, and has also served as an adjunct professor at Oral Roberts University's School of Business, where he has taught three "Non-Profit Legal Issues" courses.

Dan lives in Tulsa, Oklahoma with his wife, Mary and their son Grant.